THE CIRCLE SQUARE PATTERN

The Master Key to Organizational Change

Author of The Hidden Game Revealed

John Berling Hardy

THE CIRCLE SQUARE PATTERN
THE MASTER KEY TO ORGANIZATIONAL CHANGE

iUniverse books may be ordered through booksellers or by contacting:

iUniverse
1663 Liberty Drive
Bloomington, IN 47403
www.iuniverse.com
1-800-Authors (1-800-288-4677)

ISBN: 978-1-5320-6205-6 (sc)
ISBN: 978-1-5320-6206-3 (e)

Print information available on the last page.

iUniverse rev. date: 11/21/2018

CONTENTS

PREFACE: THE GREAT DIVIDE

On the surface, our world has never seemed smaller. Instant communications, the rise of multinational corporations, and the interconnectedness of national economies would suggest that barriers are being broken down. Globalization, the media, and the power of international brands are all homogenizing the world.

The rate of change is increasing. Technological advances that once spanned centuries or even decades now take place in years or months. The world that we inhabit today moves faster and evolves more dramatically than the world of our parents.

On balance, this is a good thing. We live longer and healthier lives than ever before. We have a global self-awareness that did not exist even as recently as the twentieth century.

For organizations from small businesses to global corporations, change poses a huge challenge. Imagine a successful business being like a finely tuned machine. It may take years to get it working right—that is, profitably—and it would be nice if you could just sit back and let the machine run. But today that's simply not possible. The machine must be redesigned on a regular basis. This means that people—the ones who make the machine operate—must be flexible and imaginative. They must have substance. They must be Masters.

Those who are self-centered, rigid, and exclusionary, and see life as a sort of game of smoke and mirrors—the Players—cannot adapt to change. Like dinosaurs, they are destined for extinction. And the companies they control will inevitably become unprofitable and will collapse.

The distinction between the Masters and the Players is so great that I believe it is the defining characteristic dividing the human race into two very separate camps. It is far greater than culture, religion, geographic location, race, or gender. Those of substance speak one language, while those without it, speak quite another. There is really no conversation between the two groups.

Those lacking in substance perceive those having it as being naive, idealistic, immature, and indulgent. Conversely, people who are living their passion see those who do not as being completely inconsequent.

This schism has always existed, but today it has become wider than ever. Rarely do we find a work environment where the two groups work harmoniously together.

A healthy organization is filled with Masters. In such an organization, your work reflects your passion. The people you work with, the suppliers you buy from, and clients you sell to all must be people of substance as well.

If you don't follow this path you'll be like the Players: insecure, alone, struggling and unhappy. Whatever relations you have will be fragile and their success will be fleeting. Your relations with those around you will be superficial, and you'll always be afraid of showing weaknesses, standing out in some way, and not quite fitting in.

However, if you pursue your passion and create a community with others who pursue theirs, you build strong relationships based on who you are, not what you are. Also, you create an established market for what you produce, which will stand the test of time and only strengthen over time. You will have what we all seek—a tribe of your own!

All the pressures on the existing model are increasing. None of the inherent structural problems that led up to the 2008 economic crash have been addressed. We are fast approaching a tipping point after which we risk a total meltdown. That which is proposed in this book is congruent with the times, it is humane, and it is easy to put in place. All it requires is the courage, faith and stamina to go where we have not gone before and stay the course. Time is of the essence—something must be done, and done now!

John Berling Hardy

INTRODUCTION

Can Players create wealth? Yes, they can create extraordinary wealth. We see it in the corporate empires that exist in the industrialized West, Japan, and Korea. We see it in the powerful government bureaucracies in Russia, China, Egypt and North Korea. But as we have seen over and over again throughout history, even vast wealth can be fleeting. Huge corporations implode overnight, like Enron did. Others, like General Motors, slowly decay and become arthritic, ultimately needing life-saving intervention. Governments are shaken by revolution. When such disasters happen, the Game is over and the Players look for another casino to ply their trade.

The Game, as designed by the Players, has persisted for centuries. And always there have been, and still are, the Masters—living parallel lives, seemingly in a different universe.

In the sixteenth century Machiavelli wrote The Prince as a kind of sales brochure to promote his services to Lorenzo Medici (the Magnificent), then the ruler of Florence. In the sense that Machiavelli never got the job, the document was a failure. Nonetheless, the book has come down to us as the definitive field manual of statecraft, which for centuries has been the favorite of diplomats, politicians, and generals the world over. Machiavelli's treatise teaches us how to play the game of power and prestige—laying out the rules and supporting them with illustrations of these principles in action drawn from his own time period, the Renaissance, as well as from antiquity.

Machiavelli's basic premise is that the Game is an immutable fact of life, no different from the laws of survival in the jungle. The goal is to win the game by any means necessary; the niceties of ethics and morality are no more than stage props used to convince opponents and allies alike that the Player—the Machiavellian actor—need not be opposed on moral grounds. So while the appearance of legality and morality are key weapons in the Player's arsenal, so are deceit and trickery and the shrewd use of power.

When we think of Machiavelli's Renaissance prince—the consummate Player—it is Cesare Borgia who comes to mind. Cesare was the epitome of the cold, calculating sociopath, and many believe he was the role model upon whom the treatise was based. Cesare was the consummate game player, respecting no moral boundaries save those dictated by the rules of expediency and realpolitik.

In today's political and corporate environment, we see many would-be Cesare Borgias. Some, like Bernie Madoff, fall to ruin. But many others achieve material wealth, power, even prestige. They succeed on Wall Street, in the boardroom, and in politics. Their rate of success versus the rate of failure is great enough so that the allure of the Player lifestyle is powerful.

Of course, just as sharks only occasionally attack other sharks, Players only occasionally prey upon each other. For any Player to succeed—from Cesare Borgia to Bernie Madoff to the dynasties of executives and managers at General Motors for forty years—wealth must be extracted not from other Players but from the numberless Drones who buy into the Game the way busloads of retirees flock to the slot machines at casinos. It is the Drones who aspire to become Players. The Drones believe in the Game and are willing to sacrifice for a seat at the table. It is the Drones who flip the burgers and hustle the insurance policies and grease the wheels for the Players' revenue machine. And, just like the slot machines that are programmed to pay out ninety cents for every dollar wagered, Drones become winners often enough to keep the vision of success alive in the heart of every other Drone. The bells ring, the lights flash, the slot machine disgorges a pile of cash onto the faux-Persian carpet of the casino, and every Drone in the room becomes infused with enthusiasm and hope: "Yes, I can be a winner, too!" With renewed energy they pump more tokens into the slot machines, while the casino managers—the Players—haul sacks of Drone cash down to the vaulted counting rooms. They know that for every Drone who walks away a winner, ten more will have gambled away their children's college educations.

Likewise, for every Drone who breaks through the barrier and ascends to the exalted realms of the Players, thousands more ride the subway to work every day and dutifully contribute to their 401(k) plans and are grateful to escape the rounds of corporate layoffs that, like the deadly blade in Edgar Allan Poe's "The Pit and the Pendulum," swing ever closer.

When an organization is controlled by Players and populated by hapless Drones, we may call it Mesozoic, in honor of the Age of Dinosaurs, the period between 245 million years ago when dinosaurs first emerged and 66 million years ago when they suddenly became extinct. Indeed, the Mesozoic era was populated by all the familiar archetypes: the predatory Tyrannosaurus Rex (the perfect Player), the lumbering Brontosaurus, and the stubborn horned Triceratops. Yet for all their power, they were unable to adapt to changing conditions, and were doomed to extinction.

The Mesozoic universe of Players and Drones may be depressing and grim, but there is hope: Players do not have a monopoly on success. Around the same period in history as Cesare Borgia, only a few miles away in the province of Marche, a very different kind of prince lived and thrived— Federico da Montefeltro, Duke of Urbino.

Federico, as a mercenary captain, is without equal in military history. Victorious in all of his military campaigns, he was never defeated in battle—a particularly notable achievement when we consider the fact that these were internecine conflicts with mercenaries employed on both sides, and no general could rely upon a sustainable advantage in terms of technology or the quality of their troops.

From all the treasures he amassed from his marshal success, Federico created a palace that was the envy of all the Renaissance princes for its beauty and elegance. His most prized treasure was a library that was reputed to be the greatest in Christendom at the time.

How was Federico able to succeed without falling into the moral tar pit of the Player? He was what we call a Master—an actor whose skills are in fact far beyond that of the Player.

The Master operates within a moral universe, builds wealth with integrity, enjoys the support of the community, and leaves a positive legacy.

How is it that Machiavelli, who must have had intimate knowledge of the exploits of the Duke of Urbino, finds no place to mention him in The Prince? Why is it that Cesare Borgia—the Player—is known by so many, yet Federico da Montefeltro—the Master—is known by so few? This book attempts to suggest a plausible answer to these questions. In the process, my aim is to cast some light on how we came to be where we are, and the changes that we need to make to our prevailing approach to leadership and organization moving forward.

This book, like The Prince, suggests a way of dealing with the world as we find it, rather than as we wish it to be. But unlike The Prince, my contention is that there is a way in which one can play—and win—the Game without selling one's soul. Players live day-to-day and see only as far as the next quarter, and the rigid Circle Square Pattern that they inhabit can, like the dinosaurs, be wiped out by the unrelenting pace of change. We have seen it happen, and unless we take action it will happen over and over again.

Instead of aspiring to become Players so that we can take our place in their petrified hierarchy, we become Masters, able to turn the Game back upon itself.

1. THE IDEAL ORGANIZATION

By using the word "ideal," it may seem as though I am envisioning an organization that does not exist, or for which there is no template, thus contradicting my assertion that, like Machiavelli, we need to understand the world not as we wish it to be but as it exists today. In approaching this problem, we are challenged to simultaneously define our goal—the ideal organization—and identify an existing example.

Organizations are made up of individuals. Individuals, by their nature, possess a dual nature: they are dedicated to the success of the organization and they are dedicated to their own personal success. To varying degrees, these drives may be in conflict or they may be in harmony, depending upon the balance of each. For example, in a colony of honeybees, there is an astounding lack of "self-centeredness." Bees completely suppress any trace of individuality for the common good. They work together without internal conflict. It is to this model that military organizations aspire - to be a collection of individual actors who are all "on the same page" and who, without intellectualizing or seeking personal gain, act together as one organic whole.

At the opposite spectrum, one may point to Wall Street investors, who, while they act as a group in a common arena, are Players driven purely by self-interest and, if it were not for the fear of prosecution, would gleefully cheat each other. They know no common goal, only the individual goal of self-enrichment at any cost.

The Antwerp Diamond Market

We seek a model of an organization that has achieved an organic balance between the drive for individual self-enrichment (an excess of which leads to decadence and criminality) and the beehive model of drone behavior (which leads to rigidity and stagnation). In fact, this balanced model has been in continuous existence for some five hundred years in Flanders, in the old diamond market in Antwerp.

To the uninformed bystander the market appears to be nothing more than another immaculately restored square in the old town, not noticeably different from any of those around it. Meanwhile, walking to and fro across the square in plain view to all, messengers in the traditional orthodox long black robes of the Orthodox Jews convey millions of dollars of uncut diamonds in small pouches tucked in their pockets. Only the speed of their gait and the severity of their demeanor reveal any hint of their purpose. The physical security of the market is provided by undercover police, who are disguised as shopkeepers, shoppers, a pair of lovers sitting at a café, etc. When the messengers meet, pouches are exchanged, with each then proceeding on their way. No paper changes hands; no inspection of the merchandise takes place—it is all done on trust.

The invisibility of the security measures makes it very difficult for any would-be thieves to assess how well the market is secured. The fact that all the diamond merchants belong to families who have been in this business for centuries and whose entire livelihood depends on their maintaining the absolute trust of their peers ensures that none are tempted by the short-term gain that might be had by overstating the contents of their sacks.

The Antwerp diamond market is the model of perfect control without restrictions. It is formless form, precisely what controls should be. The flow of transactions is completely fluid, without compromising security. During the centuries that this market has been in this square, great technological advances have been made in our society. We passed from the agricultural through the industrial, into the electronic and information ages. Nonetheless, this low-tech marketplace remains unsurpassed in the world in terms of its efficiency, security and simplicity. This is the perfect model for any company to follow: the needs of the individual are met, while the organization is a perfect example of form following function. There are no wasted assets, no needless expenses, only the leanest possible structure that permits the organization's mission to be met.

Within their universe, the diamond merchants of Antwerp are Masters. There are no Players and there are no Drones. As individuals, they wield wealth and power judiciously. They act both in self-interest and for the common good. They do not believe in a zero-sum game; that is, they do not believe that for me to win, you have to lose. They trust each other. Mistakes and the occasional lapse into criminal behavior are dealt with discreetly. And perhaps most importantly, Players—should one or more infiltrate the community—are banished.

The Prince of Volterra

Any reasonable person, in trying to project the model of the Antwerp Diamond Exchange onto a contemporary corporation, would insist that the Antwerp model is too horizontal, and that to avoid chaos some degree of vertical beehive-like control is necessary.

Given that some vertical control is necessary, it is important to create or define a realistic template of the human overseer. Let us consider the Prince of Volterra.

Perched in the midst of the undulating Tuscan landscape, lies the walled town of Volterra. Today it is a priceless museum of Renaissance and Etruscan culture. However, its immense fortifications bear witness to the fact that in days of yore it was a powerful city-state. Life in the town has a beautiful, even tempo. People are dressed elegantly, but not ostentatiously. All have their own style, yet it all blends together in a very pleasing tableau.

The city and its people emanate balance and harmony. People greet one another in the street.

In the middle of the town is an obscure little gateway that opens to an ancient stone path leading up a gradual slope and then turning sharply at the top. Once at the top, you discover yourself to be in a beautiful, expansive park. The topography of the park is gentle and undulating with a slight swell in the center. As you look outwards from that small hillock you can see the hills of Tuscany stretching toward the horizon in all directions. The park cannot be seen from the town, nor does one see the town from the park.

I always imagined the Prince of Volterra living in this park. He would spend his time in quiet reverie; every couple of days, he would disguise himself as a typical town dweller, descend the steps of the ancient path towards the gateway, and wait for an opportune moment, when no one was watching, to enter the town. There would typically be no real purpose to his visit, other than to pleasurably pass the time, in the process observing the general tempo of life. If he should spot something amiss—witness someone mistreating another, or sense some tension beneath the surface as he spoke with one of the townspeople—he would make careful note of it in his mind. Later, upon his return, he would have his agents discover the cause of the discord. Then, in the deftest manner, the situation would be restored to balance. The townspeople would be none the wiser for what took place; it would be as if the situation naturally resolved itself.

The Prince of Volterra is an authentic leader. The job of the authentic leader of a company is the most difficult and least rewarded there is. He or she operates quietly, with little fanfare. It is "egoless" leadership. The Prince of Volterra does not care from where comes a good idea; he does not care about the source of a mistake. All he cares about is maintaining a state of positive harmony in his town. Creativity and innovation are encouraged; generosity is rewarded; mistakes are gently corrected. Players are not tolerated.

The authentic or true leader carries responsibility for the welfare of all those in their charge. This implies caring about them as living, breathing human beings whose aspirations, concerns, and passions, become his or her own. For as long as there is a single individual within the company whose dignity is not respected, who cannot adequately provide for their family, the leader has not done their job.

By contrast the performance of a false leader is quite the opposite—one has little to do other than manage perceptions and devise ever-new accounting policies to increase one's bonuses. The false leader is concerned with getting credit; with appearing to be in charge; with asserting managerial authority; with eliminating rivals; and with flattering those above him or her in the organization.

Regrettably, organizations and corporations around the world are full of false leaders who are concerned only with avoiding mistakes and receiving credit for any positive development. They are Players, myopic individuals who see only as far as the next quarter or bonus period. They are concerned only with short-term gains and they exhibit a peculiar set of contradictory traits: they are fearful of setting long-term goals and sticking to them; they are rigid in their beliefs; and yet they are eager to embrace dubious schemes that promise short-term profits.

Regrettably, the recent history of some segments of U.S. corporate society reveals the corrosive influence of Players. This is perhaps no more starkly illustrated than the contrast, from 1970 to 2010, of the performance of General Motors versus Toyota. For forty years the Mesozoic GM was in the grip of Players: executives who were blinded by past success; rigid in their thinking; incapable of long-term planning; concerned only with their personal enrichment; and arrogant in their relationships with customers, workers, and suppliers. At GM, if you were not a Player, you were a Drone. As a Drone, your job was to shut up, follow orders, put in your hours, and cash your hefty union paycheck. Thinking was for the Players.

During this same period, Toyota grew from a humble regional manufacturer to the world's number one automaker. They were Masters. They created long-term strategies that were more important than quarterly profits; they listened to customers; they did not engage in superficial marketing schemes; they fine-tuned their products over a period of years. They did not treat their line workers as Drones; managers solicited input and kept communication open.

The low point for GM came in November 2008, when CEO Rick Wagoner flew his $36 million company jet to a hearing in Washington to make his case that GM was running out of cash and needed $12 billion in taxpayer money to avoid bankruptcy. Like lumbering, overfed dinosaurs, all three Detroit CEOs—Wagoner of GM, Alan Mulally of Ford, and Robert Nardelli of Chrysler—arrived in lavish corporate jets to plead before the Senate Banking Committee. The cost of Wagoner's flight was estimated to be $20,000. This is when the Players became jokes; they were kings who wore no clothes.

But there is always hope. Players can be removed, and people can change—sometimes dramatically. Today, General Motors, like Lazarus rising from the grave, is a company transformed. Their products are innovative and quality is improving. In February 2011 GM reported net income of $4.7 billion, or $2.89 per share, for 2010, its first annual profit since 2004. Revenue for the year totaled $135.6 billion. Profits were fueled by sales in the U.S. and China, the world's largest market for car and trucks. With a good performance in 2011, the company could even reclaim the title of world's largest automaker from Toyota, and the U.S. taxpayers could recover more of the $49.5 billion they gave the company in 2009 to save it from collapse.

Is GM now in the hands of Masters? Only time will tell.

2. THE POWER/PRESSURE PARADIGM AND LINEARITY

Why do so many organizations, like the General Motors of 1970-2010, fall short of the ideal and become Mesozoic? The causes range over a wide spectrum, from lack of authentic leadership resulting in a condition where, like a jellyfish, the organization has no ability to propel itself but is swept along by the currents, to the opposite condition, which is the domination of the company by Players who exert too much control and despite ample warnings drive the great ocean liner straight into the iceberg. Not enough authentic leadership; too much autocratic leadership. A lack of structure; too much structure. A lack of long-range planning; too rigid a belief in a preconceived plan. All are recipes for disaster.

To reveal the root causes of failure we need to first examine the external and internal forces that can shape an organization that is populated not by Masters but by Players and their unwitting Drones.

Pressure

It is axiomatic in capitalist societies that competition is good. Is this necessarily so in all cases? Certainly, no competition is a bad thing—both state control and monopolies are inefficient, and reward the few at the expense of the many.

So if no competition is bad, and competition is good, then it only stands to reason that more competition can only be better. It provides consumers with more choice, and forces the producers to up their game.

The greater the competition, the greater the pressure. In the beginning, producers work better, and smarter to beat the competition. The problem starts when they run out of ways to improve their competitiveness, but the pressure within the system keeps growing. What happens next?

Sooner or later, out of sheer necessity, some of the competitors start bending or even breaking the rules. If these few are successful in avoiding detection, the others will be compelled to follow suit if they wish to avoid falling behind. Ultimately, the situation arises where Players and Drones alike are left with a simple choice—break the rules and risk the penalty, or stick to the straight and narrow, and go under.

For example, take the 2010 British Petroleum (BP) oil spill in the Gulf. This is very likely what lay behind the scenario that led to the disaster. The drilling company was ordered to increase capacity. Wishing to remain in business, they complied. The person at BP demanding the increase was no doubt under similar pressure, and this would then carry all the way up the line to the top. In the pressure-driven environment the ultimatum presented to all those in positions of authority is: do what it takes, or we will find someone else who will.

This paying forward of pressure cannot go on interminably. Sooner or later it comes up against an immovable object—in this case Mother Nature herself. Singling out one of the links in the chain, and attempting to attribute blame to it is a complete waste of time. Once the decision to deep-sea drill was made, an irreversible chain of events was set in motion that could have but one final outcome—disaster. We cannot know which rig will be the one to fail, or when it will fail, but that some rig somewhere will cause a catastrophic failure is almost guaranteed.

We can improve technology, tighten regulations, but so long as the pressure keeps building and building we can only expect more of the same. What was deemed as an acceptable risk turned out to be unacceptable. How many other similar decisions have been made, where risks are high, corruption is systemic, creating a veritable time bomb just waiting to explode?

Control

The moment we think of the word "control," we think in terms of keeping something in check. The implied assumption is that the only way to keep things from going off course is that we must keep a close eye on the process every step of the way. Conventional thinking says that the easiest way to spot deviation is by comparing individual performance against an unchanging matrix. The only way to do this is to create a rigid structure into which individuals must fit, often by adaptation.

The problems with this approach are the following:

<u>High Cost</u> – If we wish to truly control a process we must build an extensive control system. This requires a significant initial investment, as well as a considerable commitment in time and resources in order to keep it current.

<u>Catch-Up Mode</u> – As the business environment shifts, there is inevitably going to be a lag while the system is catching up to changes in the market. This means that the company, instead of being ahead of the curve, is always in a catch-up mode. The tighter and more elaborate the control structure, the greater this lag is likely to be, and the greater the investment in continuously updating the process.

<u>Contra-Selection</u> – A restrictive command-control structure tends to attract certain types of individuals and repel others. It creates a conformist culture that promotes those who are either compliant in nature and can be relied upon to do as they are told, or those who are adept impression managers, skilled at corporate politics. Meanwhile, the organization experiences a brain drain, as those who are innovative, or stand out in any way, are crowded out of the work force.

<u>Efficiency vs. Effectiveness</u> – This type of environment can very often appear to be efficient because of the narrow and restrictive way in which productivity is defined. Everyone is terribly busy, but busy doing the wrong things.

<u>Rigidity</u> – The organization becomes very set in its ways as the supply chain becomes grooved within very narrowly defined parameters. This makes it difficult to accommodate the varied and changing requirements of consumers in today's market environment. The firm is then placed at a severe disadvantage in relation to more nimble and flexible competitors in the industry.

<u>Silo Effect</u> – The linear command control structure creates a silo effect through which communication generally travels from top down, and does not cross highly defined geographical and functional boundaries. In a continuously changing environment, problems require a multifaceted approach involving the whole organization, not just the resources of a single unit that is highly defined both functionally and geographically.

Having established that this rigid structure is artificial, archaic, and requires a great investment in time and resources to maintain, why does it persist? Is there a dynamic within the organization, hidden beneath the surface, which holds this rigid structure in place?

Linearity vs. Relationship

The Power/Pressure Paradigm reflects the inevitable organic evolution that an organization populated by Players and Drones undergoes when subjected to competitive market forces. Instead of becoming flexible and resilient, the pressured Mesozoic organization becomes rigid and brittle. It references only itself and its past accomplishments. It recycles solutions to old problems. It is threatened by change. It sees progress not as evolutionary but as linear - a revenue graph that must always go up.

What is the alternative? When we study organizations populated by Masters – such as the Antwerp Diamond Exchange – they demonstrate a highly developed understanding of relationship. They see themselves and the world around them as a single integrated entity. In fact, the relationship paradigm would be as self-evident to them as the linear paradigm is to us.

The relationship paradigm is far more congruent with the way our minds work than is the linear paradigm. If we picture the world in terms of intersecting energy fields, it becomes immediately evident that the linear model simply no longer applies. There is a collection of theories developed in the various fields of science over the last century, referred to collectively as Chaos theory, which provides a much better fit.

Chaos theory posits that there exists a hidden pattern, beyond the perception of our senses, which guides the course of events. The world is viewed as a network of interconnected systems. Rather than being attached to one another in any kind of sequence, each one has a direct connection to all the others. Similarly, within each system all the constituent elements are fully integrated as well.

Change within the system is not sequential, but global. That is to say that instead of the domino effect predicted by the linear paradigm, change in any part of the system would instantaneously influence the entire system.

It is not unlike "flocking," which is the breathtaking effect demonstrated by birds when, in a flock of hundreds or even thousands of individuals, they wheel and glide in the sky as if they were one organism. This behavior is called herding in quadrupeds, and shoaling or schooling in fish. The behavior of schooling fish is not linear; indeed, if it were, the school's attempt to evade the predator would be pathetically slow and individuals could be easily picked off.

It is not unlike a parade of highly trained soldiers who move in lockstep as if they were one organism. But the soldiers are controlled by a commanding officer in a strict hierarchy. If the commanding officer were to be suddenly absent, chaos would result. Flocking birds require no commanding officer.

Each system has an inherent tolerance to change. It can absorb a certain magnitude of disturbance without losing its basic structural integrity. It does this by continuously compensating for change in one area with a series of adjustments in other parts of the system. It is analogous to a man riding a unicycle: the rider can absorb little inconsistencies in the terrain, or the odd gentle nudge, however should they be pushed sufficiently severely, they will lose their balance completely. Similarly, if the Mesozoic system is disrupted beyond a certain tolerance it will collapse.

The current economic crisis may be just this type of disturbance. To the extent that it has spread to engulf the whole world, impacting not just the North American financial sector but de-stabilizing the entire world economy, it may well have gone past the point where any corrective measure can avert a total meltdown. If this is the case we will find ourselves in a "too little, too late" scenario. Once a certain critical mass has been reached, that is to say, the structure of the system has been sufficiently compromised the process becomes irreversible. At this point, there is nothing to do but stand by and watch events unfold.

At the point of collapse, one of two things can happen. Either the system will spontaneously reorganize itself into a new system, which has a new set of dynamics, or it will simply disintegrate.

Returning to the image of the unicycle, as seen from the vantage of a casual observer, the rider's fall will appear to be a progression of events, starting from the push, to wavering, to flailing, to falling. Nevertheless, in reality there was a specific point at which the balance was irrevocably broken, after which the fall became inevitable.

Let us now apply this same set of principles to the progression from thought to action. During the decision-making process, the course of action decided upon no longer falls within the realm of choice, but has become inevitable after a point of no return. In this sense, the actions we observe and react to are really the echoes of the decisions that have preceded them. It is similar to when we look up into the sky the stars we see may no longer actually exist, as the picture conveyed to us by our eyes is a depiction of something that took place millions of years ago.

The implication is that those who live in the linear paradigm with its emphasis on concrete reality are always finding themselves closing the barn door after the horses have left the stable. They create new regulations in response to events, rather than stopping and thinking about where things are likely to have moved in the interlude between when the event was initiated and when it came to our attention, as well the direction in which they are likely to move in the future.

Similarly, right and wrong cannot be determined in any prescriptive way by referring to a fixed set of laws. Each situation will be the result of a unique combination of influences. Therefore, even when we allow for the existence of "good" or "evil," we cannot definitively determine such acts as murder or theft, to be categorically right, or wrong.

An illustration of this point comes from the book Les Misérables by Victor Hugo. The protagonist, Jean Valjean, an escaped convict, seeks refuge in the home of a priest. The priest treats him kindly, giving him food and lodging. In the night, the fugitive steals off, helping himself to a pair of silver candlesticks belonging to the priest. Later the same night, the man is apprehended by the police who bring him back to the home of the priest. Upon asking the priest to identify the man who stole his property, he states that the candlesticks were given to the man as a gift. This gesture of kindness makes such a strong impression upon Val jean that it changes the course of his life.

Juxtaposed against the priest is a police inspector who hounds Val jean from the time of his escape from prison, determined to make him pay his rightful debt to society. The more good things Val jean does for others, the more he achieves, and the higher he rises in society, the greater the inspector's obsession with bringing him down becomes.

No application of linear logic could support the priest's actions. Valjean has repaid his kindness with theft. Probability would dictate that the convict would go on to commit still more crimes in the future. The priest's actions were guided by love and faith—two qualities that lie outside the boundaries of the linear paradigm. There is no deductive process that rationally justifies kindness. There is no logical argument that supports faith.

In a world run by men such as the priest, there will be theft, sloppiness and chaos. In the Mesozoic world ruled by the inspectors, there will be order, crime will be contained, and justice will be meted out to those who deserve it. However, which world would we rather live in? Speaking for myself, I would far prefer a chaotic hell to a sterile heaven.

Linearity is the myth behind all the others. It defines our reality. It is the master key to the matrix. By unraveling it, by debunking it, exposing it as artificial constructs, instead of "the way it is," we can finally break loose from the matrix. Now, we can proceed to unravel all the other myths, which we have become attached to, and in so doing, start to think for ourselves.

The Challenges of the Post-Crisis World

Today's business environment is fast paced, chaotic, and unpredictable. The one constant confronting the senior management of any organization in the world today is continuous, unrelenting change. In order to respond to this environment every company requires the following:

1. A continuous and reliable flow of **feedback from the marketplace** that enables management to address current market needs as well as anticipate future trends.
2. A **flexible supply chain** that can accommodate and anticipate continuously changing needs.
3. A committed, flexible, **innovative work force** that is in tune with the outer environment.
4. An effective, **informal information network** that is able to apply know-how and information from different functional and geographical areas to specific challenges confronting the company.

DIAGRAM 1: THE MODERN BUSINESS ENVIRONMENT

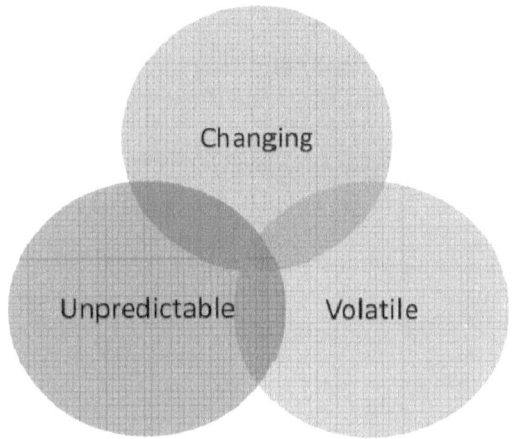

The current Control-Pressure Paradigm (CPP) fails all the criteria outlined above. Later in the book in the section on the Circle Square Pattern (CSP) we will examine how and why that is the case. But first let us explore a certain social dynamic, one that exists in every social environment, that is mentioned in the Book of Genesis, yet seems to slip below the radar.

This is the dynamic between the Players and the Masters.

This dynamic does not take place within a vacuum. It exists within a broader context. This context includes culture and the times we live in. This takes us to our next topic—the Cult of Marketing.

3. THE CULT OF MARKETING

If I were to suggest to you that you the reader are a member of a cult, you would be shocked, angered, even enraged. Of course, if you were to approach any religious fundamentalist, Scientologist or Moonie and pose the same question, you would get pretty much the same reaction. The only real difference between their cult and ours is its size—theirs number in the thousands, and tens of thousands, while ours number in the millions. Ours is the cult of marketing! It is the veneer over today's variation of the Game.

Selling, Persuasion, and Manipulation

What is selling exactly? It is getting someone to buy something—anything! It can be a radio, a dental procedure, even ourselves. The word "getting" can just as easily be replaced by the words "persuading," "inducing," "coercing," or "manipulating." All of these will get the job done—the word selected depends very much upon our own perspective.

Natural salespersons will choose persuasion as the descriptor. Those of us who are introverts or might be seen by our peers as refusniks, will be more drawn to the darker end of the spectrum, characterizing selling as manipulation or coercion. It is interesting to note that almost any motivational course you are likely to listen to, will, at some point, will include a distinction between persuasion and manipulation. The distinction will go something like this: "Persuasion is for the benefit of the consumer, while manipulation is only for the benefit of the seller. Manipulation is only short lived, and will inevitably lead to buyer's remorse; whereas persuasion will lead to a strong relationship between buyer and seller which will yield benefit to both parties, not just now, but in the future as well."

For thousands of years, religious leaders, politicians, entrepreneurs, army generals, and seductresses have used manipulation. It has successfully kept entire populations bamboozled for generations. Therefore, the very notion that it is short lived and doomed to fail is farcical. In fact, only a salesperson would ever buy into such a pitch.

Human beings are driven by emotion, not reason. More can be achieved by a manipulative appeal to an audience's emotional weaknesses than with the most cogent, brilliant argument. Being a master manipulator is the key success factor in being an effective marketer/salesman. Manipulation is the art of managing impressions. It stands to reason then, that through the process of natural selection, those who are the most talented at impression management rise to the top of the selling profession. These are the Players.

Branding

In the Wild West, ranchers commonly herded their cattle together. The best way to identify which cow belonged to whom was to brand the cattle. Can you imagine being one of those cows and willingly, enthusiastically, branding yourself? Well that is exactly what we have done to ourselves.

Everyone is forced to think of themselves as a brand. No matter what your particular gift or expertise happens to be, you have no choice but to play their Game. Our ability to sell our brand becomes the key to success. In a world where the marketer is king, talking a good game, looking good, being likeable, being sexy become the winning traits. Knowledge, integrity, fortitude, kindness, generosity, and graciousness become nothing more than frills, mere anachronisms. They are the traits associated with those on the fringe—the losers, artists, intellectuals, the has-beens. In fact, substance of any kind becomes a burden. It is ballast that holds you down, limiting your creativity in concocting what is to be presented to the client.

If you are a homebuilder, your success is no longer driven by the quality of homes you build, but your ability to project an image of competence and integrity. Similarly, dentists, doctors, and accountants can no longer rely upon excellence and hard work to create a thriving practice.

Talking, rather than doing, becomes the key success factor. In fact, this is so much the case, that to the extent that, anyone is directly involved in the creation of the goods or service they provide rather than its promotion, they are looked down upon. In this way, the talents of the truly gifted are marginalized and the Players are able to steer the Game in their favor. It is no surprise then, to see that professional firms; management consulting, architects, lawyers, are controlled by the "rainmakers"—the partners who are skilled in bring in the clients.

We commonly speak about reinventing ourselves. Using the word reinvent in place of re- package is far more than a benign choice in terminology. It reflects an entire worldview. It is as if, instead of being single unified beings, we are a bundle of interchangeable traits, which could be mixed and matched to suit the demands of the market.

Turning us into "brands" encourages us to see other people as either potential customers we can sell to, or as salesmen who wish to sell to us. Seeing each other in this way makes us suspicious of one another as we find ourselves unable to take any statement at face value and must constantly seek some ulterior motivation in all our interactions with others. Associations and alliances, which are entirely motivated by self-interest, crowd out authentic relationship. In place of human beings forming authentic relationships with one another, we are only able to interact with one another within the narrow confines of our own brands.

As the process continues, selling no longer becomes a choice; it becomes a matter of survival. The market becomes inundated with hustlers. Lacking any objective, reliable criteria upon which to assess competence; likeability and slickness become the key success criteria. In this way, the buyer is steered unwittingly towards the con men. Meanwhile, those who cannot sell are simply invisible.

Placed in this context, the success of investment bankers in conveying an air of success and competence is easy to understand. Their showmanship became a self-fulfilling prophecy; the well-tailored suit, the perfectly coifed hair, the confident, even demeanor- all convey success, competence and authority. This then, forms the backdrop for what they are selling: the opportunity to be rich, successful and popular, like they appear to be. By the time they actually make their pitch, the potential buyer is already sold. Who is the perspective buyer? Anyone in the room!

The very omnipresence of the Game places us all in the position of having to choose between two options, one more repugnant than the other. The first option is to bite the bullet and attempt to sell. Unfortunately, when it comes to mastering bluff and small talk, we are like fish out of water. Not being natural liars, we are no match for those who are naturally inclined to embellishment and hyperbole. Now we are caught between a rock and a hard place. Instead of simply getting on with the business at hand, we spend all our free time going to sales courses, and listening to motivational tapes, in the hope that a few crumbs of wisdom will fall our way.

If we are not socially skilled, we have to ally ourselves with a rainmaker. To add insult to injury, in the event that we are successful in finding such a hustler, we become the drone, the weaker party in the relationship. Over time, our confidence erodes, and eventually we fall victim to despair, or some form of sedation.

Players are born with an innate understanding of the gullibility of human nature. They know that we all need to be liked, need to feel successful, need to feel that our peers look up to us. They nonchalantly look on as the wheel turns like a giant merry-go-round. They are in no hurry, because they know that the axis, around which this wheel is turning, is fixed. Sometimes they spin the wheel slowly, sometimes quickly, but it is always fixed in one place. It is never going anywhere. Those on the merry-go-round are under the illusion that they are moving rapidly toward their goals, their dreams, and their destinies. Meanwhile, those turning the wheel know that nobody, including themselves, is going anywhere.

Collapse is built into the model. This spinning wheel has to spin faster and faster to maintain its equilibrium. Eventually it has maxed out; terminal velocity is reached. From that point on, it is only a matter of time before it breaks.

As the economy heats up, it reaches saturation, at which point most of us have multiple TVs, cars, a home, as well as the essentials in life. If the wheel were left to turn of its own accord at this point, it would begin to slow down. Those who engineered the Game need to do something to keep increasing the speed of the spin. Now comes the coup de grace—a kind of alchemy that transforms wants into needs, choice into compulsion, and creates a buying frenzy!

By turning us into narcissistic, ravenous junkies, and then enabling our addiction with easy credit, the merry-go-round becomes a kind of self-propelling mechanism, a man-made whirlwind that is perpetually accelerating. Once this process is set in motion, all the Players need do is to sit back and watch the great wheel spin, knowing full well that sooner or later it will fall off its axis—and when it does, they will walk away and let others sort through the wreckage.

Over the last several decades, increasing numbers of products have been foisted upon the public. At first, these addressed real needs. However, over time, as needs gave way to wants, and credit was made readily available, the boundaries of what the market would bear were removed. Consumption became rapacious. Consequently, within the company, while the contributions made by operations and administration remained finite, the potential contribution made by sales became limitless, the inevitable result being that almost all businesses today are marketing/sales driven.

This entire focus upon making the sale, with next to no thought upon delivering the product, is not sustainable in the long run. The current banking crisis is a prime example of the Game run amuck.

DIAGRAM 2: KEY SUCCESS FACTORS FOR ADVANCEMENT

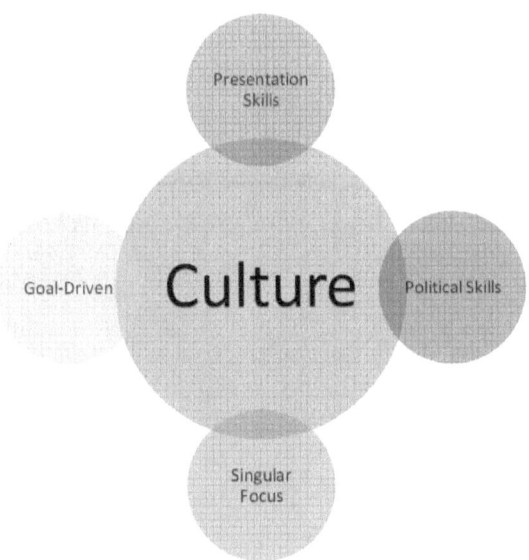

What goes up must come down. The enormous bubble created by the sales/marketing driven economy finally burst. On a certain level, this collapse did not come as a complete surprise to any of us. Nonetheless, when it did come, its brutal reality, the chaos and the carnage, was a major shock for us all.

Every culture has its winners and losers—the winners being those who thrive in the system and the losers being those who cannot seem to fit in or get with the program. Who are the winners and losers likely to be in an organizational environment dominated by the Cult of Marketing and the Control-Pressure Paradigm?

4. PLAYERS, DRONES, AND MASTERS

Chris is sitting in his downtown apartment reading in his bathrobe. It is ten o'clock on a Tuesday morning. He spots an ad for someone seeking financing for a new venture. As Chris reads the ad, he notices from the wording that they are not native English speakers. He takes a sip of this coffee, turns to me and says, "Johnny, read this ad. What do you see?"

I take a quick glance at the ad. "It's pretty straightforward," I say. "Some guys looking for money for a new venture." Then I return the question: "What do you see, Chris?"

"What I see," Chris replies, "is an investor; a foreigner; probably Chinese or Arab. He's looking to find a local silent partner." The sub-text in Chris's mind, which is not shared with me, is that he has spotted his next mark.

Chris would present himself as a "go-to" guy; someone who knows people and gets things done. He would take a prospect to his law firm and introduce them to some of his partners. On the wall in his office is a picture of Chris shaking hands with the Governor-General. The firm itself is real enough. Chris's connection to it, however, is somewhat embellished. Chris's only connection to the firm is an understanding that he can use their corner office and boardroom and represent himself as a partner, in return for the promise of business likely to come their way.

Chris is a Player. His specialty is separating the beneficiaries of trust funds from their money. He does not lie; he embellishes. He does not steal; he skims off the top. As the rest of the world is racing to complete their daily to do lists, get ahead, or simply get by, Chris is watching the whole spectacle, taking ostentatiously long puffs on his Cuban cigar. He has no real ambition, other than to live well and be entertained. He takes what he wants and leaves the rest.

A con man is the master of misdirection. He creates rapport, and credibility through an effusive, engaging manner and strategic name-dropping. As we come to like him and be impressed by his impressive array of connections, we find ourselves swept up by his charm and energy. At the same time, we are flattered by the attention that this "important" person is paying to us. He speaks with a pleasant, even cadence. He speaks and he speaks and he speaks. Before we can fully absorb one piece of information, we are already presented with another. In this way, we are kept continuously off balance; but we do not know it. This is the art of the con.

The longer this process goes on, the more addicted we become to the excitement and the positive reflection of our own vanity. The claims made by the con men become progressively more exaggerated, even absurd. The more we believe, the more we wish to believe. At the same time, something else is happening. This is the mechanism driving the con. Our emotional investment in this person being who they claim to be, only increases over time. By extension, the pain and humiliation we will experience in discovering that we have been duped and played for fools increases as well. This, then, is the anatomy of the con. Be it a cult leader, a salesperson, a stock promoter, or a politician, the basic template is the same. It is insultingly simple; but it works.

DIAGRAM 3: THE PLAYER PERSONALITY PROFILE

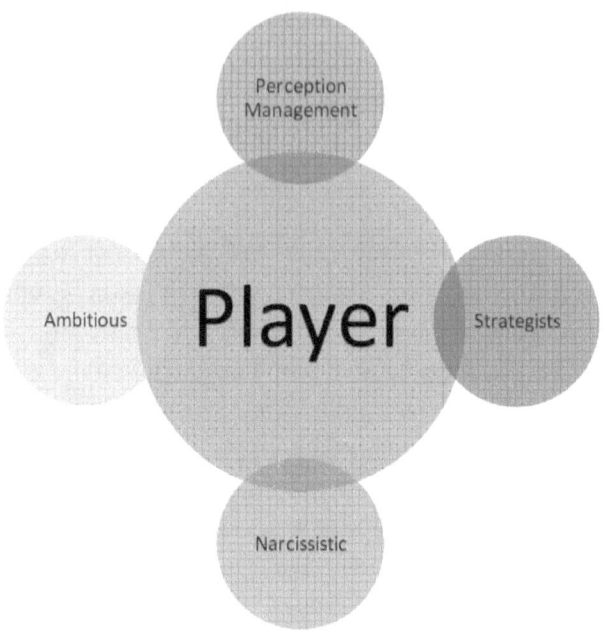

The Three Aspects of Players

The Player is someone for whom life is a game. Most of us have a Player aspect within us; it comes to the fore when we are participating in competitive sport or playing cards. The distinction between the average person and the Players is that for the Player, the game never ends; it extends to every aspect of their lives. Be it in the boardroom, around the water cooler at work, with their buddies at the pub, or at home with their own family, their game-face is always on. This Game metaphor is an excellent one for describing the Player personality. It has three aspects:

1. Natural Actor

The first aspect is that of the Player in a theatrical troupe—an actor. Similar to the actor, they are masters at managing the impressions they create on the audience, as well as managing how the audience perceives the message they're conveying. The success of the theatrical actor depends very much on their ability to sell the audience on the credibility of the character they are playing. In real life, this translates to succeeding in having others buy into what they are selling, be it a product, an investment opportunity, or a service.

2. Skilled Manipulator

The second sense of Player is in the context of one who plays others. Players are naturally skilled at uncovering the deeper motivations and weaknesses of their peers, and then preying upon them. The Player will rarely show his or her hand; the victim thinks all along that he or she has made a free choice.

3. Ruthless Competitor

Finally, we have the game aspect of the Player. Seeing life as a game in all instances precludes there ever being a win-win solution. To the Player there are no compromises that are lasting; lip service may be paid to negotiating agreements with others, but this is only in order to lull the other into a false sense of security. Beneath the surface, the Player always remains focused on their initial objective. It is their very relentlessness that makes them so phenomenally successful.

Impression Management

The key to success in any game is to be able to influence, or control, events so that they fall in one's favor. To this end, the Player's modus operandi is to achieve and maintain leverage over their opponent. Just like holding the higher ground in a battle, leverage helps the Player to maintain the upper hand in the relationship. This is true if the Player is an executive in a corporation seeking to amass more power and a promotion, or if he or she is an independent operator like Chris.

This leverage need not be real; usually it is enough that it is merely perceived. Therefore, bluffing, or impression management, is an integral part of the Game.

There is an Italian expression: "fare una bella figura," which roughly translates to "putting on a nice face." This encapsulates this sentiment quite succinctly. Rather than being based upon objective reality, the focus shifts to the appearance of reality. Society rewards the appearance of virtue, rather than virtue itself. The people who appear to be nice, appear to be intelligent, and appear to be competent, are those who thrive in today's society. The executives who appear to be working hard are those who get promoted. The surface is what counts. What doesn't show doesn't matter!

The poseurs, who always existed and thrived throughout history, have never done so in such numbers. Whereas previously they were the exception, now they have become the rule. It starts with projecting an air of success. Then, when we buy into "them" as a product, we proceed to buy whatever it is they are pushing. In this way, appearing to be successful becomes the only real qualification for success. With this edict, the circle is complete, and impression management has now become an end in and of itself.

In the inverted world of the Game, the best and the brightest are crowded out by the imposters. The Players take the spotlight and do their best to marginalize the others. Those who are actually talented or show any signs of real competence become the witnesses who know too much. They are, by their very existence, a threat to the status quo and the Players will not hesitate to remove them from the playing field, by whatever means necessary, should the need arise.

As described earlier, these conspiracies of the weak to usurp the strong, will never reveal themselves for what they are. They will be cloaked in prudence, respect for tradition, and will manipulate our innate fear of the new, of the unknown, to support it.

Those virtual people cannot completely rid themselves of those who are the genuine article, because someone is required to actually produce. Consequently, a small number of these dinosaurs are allowed to stay and on occasion, are very well remunerated, and given impressive titles, but never under any circumstances are they given any real power. They may become experts, advisers, or researchers, but they are always well removed from where any real power resides.

The newest apex predator in the Game is the kind of investment bankers that have occupied the headlines as of late. Their credo is wanton hedonism—flaunting the spoils of success, beautiful cars, lovers and other toys. This new type of Superman no longer even bothers paying lip service to niceness and fair play. They are instead the barbarians at the gate. The image they project is tough, brash, and lean, with the philosophy of "take no prisoners." Like the character Gordon Gekko, they cheerfully boast that greed is good.

Are the Players really competent in their fields? Are they the paragons of the excellence of which they so eloquently speak? Are they even the brass-balled alphas they portray themselves to be? They may indeed be masters! However, their mastery is of an altogether different sort.

They have mastered the appearance of competence, integrity; and all those virtues they so eloquently speak of. These Players profess their virtues, and profess them loudly. They are delusional. Yet their delusions are seductive. As we experience their boundless confidence, we unwittingly find ourselves believing them. After all, they must be competent. They must have integrity. Otherwise, how could they be so incredibly sure of themselves? They drive nice cars, wear nice suits, and they have this air of success about them. Everybody else believes them to be winners. Who are we to doubt them? Even if we were to speak out against them, it would only look like sour grapes on our part. And, so it goes.

General Characteristics of the Player

Nunzio is an electrician, or more precisely, a master electrician, as he will tell you. He arrives at the job site in a shiny, late-model pick-up truck. His truck is white and always immaculate. When Nunzio arrives on the site, he takes the time to finish his cell phone call, in a leisurely fashion, and then emerges from the truck, in a relaxed leisurely fashion. Nunzio is wearing designer jeans, designer boots, and a fitted sports jacket. From what I have described so far, you might think that Nunzio is an ass. This is, no doubt a fair description of Nunzio, however there is something about Nunzio which is infectious. One cannot help liking Nunzio.

After the sales meeting, during which he stresses personal service to his clients, as his winning formula, you are not likely to hear from him until it is time for a progress payment. Despite being a master electrician, Nunzio devotes his time to selling and collecting exclusively.

I have known Nunzio for several years. One of his favorite lines is, "Johnny, I've got your back." But over the years, one thing I have come to count on is that anytime I really do need Nunzio, he will give me a compelling reason why he cannot do what I am asking of him. At least, not right then. Despite this, in his own mind, Nunzio is fully convinced that he has had my back for a long time, for which he is owed a debt of gratitude. Gratitude is a bit of a bête noir for Nunzio. He spends a lot of time dwelling on how much he does for others and how little he receives in return. The construction industry is cyclical and contractors are going out of business all the time. Many truly worthy electricians close up shop. Nunzio not only endures; he thrives. Nunzio is a Player!

Players come in all shapes and sizes. They can be the Wall Street tycoon, but they can just as easily be the local real estate agent, school principal, or, as in the case of Nunzio, a electrical contractor. However, in all these examples the degree of finesse with which they ply their trade may vary, at heart they are all essentially the same. So then, what are these distinguishing features, which make the Players so different from the rest of us?

Players are born, not made. The Player is compulsive; they cannot but play. Their manipulations, their deceitfulness, their twisting and bending the truth to always reflect well on them and further their aims is more of a reflex than a conscious choice. Being a Player is not a matter of choice, but destiny.

The Player lies and manipulates with such facility that, in a very real sense, they cannot truly distinguish between fact and fiction. Their fabrications are as real for them as the veritable facts are for the rest of us. There is none among us who does not in some way bend the truth to suit. Nonetheless, even though our variations of a particular event may vary, they will not diverge completely. For a Player, the facts are the bare canvas upon which they paint masterpieces, which have only the vaguest relation to what actually took place. In a sense, the Player is as mad as a Hatter, but their particular brand of psychosis is so socially adaptive that if we were to brand them as insane, we would be indicting the entire society we live in.

One quality common to all Players worth highlighting is an absolute absence of empathy. This cannot be stressed strongly enough. To say that players lack empathy is actually a gross understatement. The Player is wholly indifferent to anyone's suffering but their own.

To the extent that another strokes their vanity, or is useful in some way, they are tolerated. If these conditions are, for whatever reason, no longer met, the other simply ceases to exist.

An example of this is their uncanny ability to stay on message, whether it is O.J. Simpson protesting his innocence, or Dick Cheney lionizing the economic record of the Bush presidency. No matter what information is provided to refute their claims, they stick to their guns to the bitter end.

As much as this sounds pathological, it actually works very much in their favor. The sheer relentlessness, with which they maintain their position, eventually makes us unsure of our own.

Players have a healthy disdain for anything approximating work. Be it creative, intellectual or menial, it is simply below them. You will always find them well away from the din of battle. They occupy themselves with selling, promoting, and marketing on the one side and with all things related to money, on the other. Anything between the two, the actual creation of the product, for instance, is of no interest to them. Being free from the pressures most of us experience in trying to meet deadlines and just keeping on keeping on, players are the picture of cool, unwavering composure—never in a rush, never flustered, and never busy.

Players are naturally drawn to wealth and power. It makes sense that those jobs, social settings and tribes with the highest status will attract the greatest concentration of Players.

In the food chain of the sub-prime crisis, the percentage concentration of Players geometrically increased as we move up from homeowner, through bankers, to investment bankers. No doubt, there were some shrewd homeowners who took advantage of the anomalies in the system, but they were in such small numbers in proportion to the whole population as to be the exception that makes the rule. Conversely, among the senior management of any of the investment banks we would be hard pressed to find someone who is not a Player. It is as if there is a critical mass of Players within a group, a tipping point, after which the entire group becomes transformed, as if by magic.

The Players' selfishness may be all-consuming, but their innate sense of social survival impels them to congregate into tribes. An excellent example of this is found in criminal organizations. Even if they would gladly slit each other's throats, they will turn their enmity towards an outsider first. Only once the outsider, the interloper, is successfully removed, will they return to jockeying for position within the tribe. Another example of this is the Afghan civil war. The tribes banded together in order to oust the invader, Russia. But once Russia was successfully defeated they once again resumed their tribal disputes, to the point that the situation degenerated into a civil war.

Players, like wolves, travel in packs. The lone wolf does not pose much of a threat. However, if encountered when in a pack, the danger becomes real and immediate. Furthermore, in the eyes of the wolf, the sheep are there for the taking. In the dualistic mind of the Player, the world is made up of wolves and sheep, and nothing in between. In their minds, if you are not a wolf you must be a sheep. If you are a sheep, you are fair game.

The Players are predators. Unapologetic, they are proud of it. As the wolf would be indifferent to the plight of sheep, so are the Players indifferent to the suffering they cause to those they have determined to be fair prey.

As a final note, it is interesting to note that the Players tolerate no loyalties that do not support their own tribe. This is because the Players' tribe has a monopoly on power and social status. Those groups that deviate from the norm in any way, or threaten the status quo, are labeled as cults, and either marginalized or completely ostracized.

Beta Players and Alpha Players

The Players, like any tribe, have their own variation of leaders and followers. The garden-variety Player is cunning and manipulative, but limited in scope. They are clever enough to navigate their way around in the day to day variations of the Game, but do not have enough intelligence to comprehend the big picture. Strategy remains the domain of the Player.

The garden-variety or Beta Player is principally driven by vanity. For these people looking good, looking successful and appearing to be in charge is everything. They are the ultimate impression managers. This means that status, conspicuous wealth, and physical attractiveness fill their horizon, effectively eclipsing anything else.

It is more the accoutrements of power than the power itself that the Betas seek. Their locus of control is external; they are constantly in need of acknowledgement and affirmation. It is not so much that they need to be stroked; they demand it as their due.

For the master, Alpha Player, their world begins and ends with power, and by extension, control. For them, it is not enough to have status and all the trappings of power; they need the real thing. Typically, given a choice between the two, they will always opt for the latter. However, in the end they are not satisfied unless they have both. The Alpha only feels comfortable when they have absolute control over events and people in their life. Suffering from the most exaggerated delusions of grandeur, they are the absolute monarchs in their inner world.

The Chinese, who have been at this Game longer than anyone else, have codified the strategies of the Alpha Players in a collection of historical parables known as the "36 Strategies." Its defining metaphor, translated literally from the Chinese, is "Thick Face, Black Heart." Interwoven within these parables is a vivid picture of the master Player.

Thick Face reflects the ability to be indifferent to how one appears to others. Others' estimation of their worth, whether they regard them as villain or hero, cowardly or courageous, are only of interest to the extent that they serve their objective. This objective, then, invariably involves the pursuit of power or glory, usually both.

Black Heart relates to the intentions and actions of the Player. As the metaphor implies, Black Heart is the ability to plumb the depths of evil and to be utterly indifferent to the ways and means enlisted to achieve the end goal. This means that there are no rules, no taboos, and no lengths that one can go to that are too repulsive to employ in the Game.

The Alpha rarely seeks the limelight, leaving it for the Beta to bask in. They see its 24/7 demands for impression management as a tiresome bore. They instead, can be found in the shadow of power, behind the scenes, only barely visible. Two of the best contemporary examples are Karl Rove and Dick Cheney. Both men pursued their objectives with single- minded determination, as well as a complete indifference to the means employed, the ethical or moral barriers crossed. Also, both were dismissive, to the point of being contemptuous, of any criticism of their actions.

In Rove's case, it was in creating a whisper campaign that implanted false innuendo about anyone deemed to be in the way. For Cheney, it was trampling on the constitutional rights of citizens, of this and future generations, shrouded by the mantle of combating terrorism. Both Cheney and Rove were indifferent to how their actions would be regarded by posterity.

Drones

As mentioned earlier, the Players have a disdain for anything resembling work. To this end, they are expert at getting others to do their dirty work and to create the wealth that Players skim like cream off the top of fresh milk. This serves them in several ways.

Firstly, by distancing themselves from the nasty business at hand, it allows them to preserve their air of moral superiority, before others as well as themselves.

Secondly, it provides protection. Drones are a limitless, fully expendable resource. In the event that things should go awry, the Players are secure in the knowledge that someone else will take the fall. To this end, they are artists at inducing others to fight their battles for them. They will never allow themselves to be drawn into a fair fight. The only time they will engage in direct confrontation, is when the odds are heavily stacked in their favor. Players, therefore, need to create a buffer. Being skilled at impression management, they invest their time and energy in manipulating others to act as their proxies.

Third, another well-concealed agenda behind the engineered reality created by the Game is the recruitment of these Drones. For the Game to function, it requires that the majority of the society must be turned into Drones, which can be relied upon to mindlessly implement policy. This extends not only to those on the front lines: bank tellers, factory workers, or clerks, but to those who are standing behind them, whip in hand: middle management.

Finally, it is the Drones, like the day laborers in South African diamond mines, who create wealth. They build the houses, forge the parts, plow the fields, teach the children in school, pump the gas, and take out the credit card loans. The Players, who control the means of production and access to capital, reap the profits.

In our present incarnation of the Game, the epitome of the Drone is the corporate trooper. Always positive and enthusiastic they operate in a very narrow emotional bandwidth. We all know these people; they have the big handshakes and the hearty laughs. No matter how much time we spend with these people, we never feel any closer to them. The degree of intimacy and familiarity always remains at the level of a person with whom we recently chatted at a cocktail party. Rather than getting the impression that they are putting on some act, one gets the sense that that is all there is. They are like those wedding cakes that are so beautiful to look at, but once you cut beneath the icing, you find an innocuous filling of bland angel cake.

The Drones' worldview is so firmly entrenched that they simply do not seem to hear anything outside their bandwidth. For example, often being rightwing fundamentalists, any talk of equality or fairness is categorized as socialism and dismissed out of hand. They deal in "hard facts." They don't like to waste time so they always need to know what is in it for them. This "what" translates into definable benefits and results. The intricacies and nuances of the "how" and "why" do not hold their attention.

These troopers are the perfect implementers to carry out corporate policy. Lacking imagination, reliably corrupt, they can be counted upon to do their jobs and not ask too many questions. In today's globalized environment, regardless of whether one is in New York or Bombay, their dress, manner, and mindset are very much the same. There is no longer any need for them to adapt to different environments, since the local culture has been paved over by the Internet and MTV.

When the Drones come to dominate the ranks of middle and upper management, the company becomes a kind of juggernaut. The uniformity of mindset makes the company reasonably effective as long as the movement is along a straight line. However, the moment that events force the company to stray from the line, the corporation encounters serious difficulty. Dealing with nuance and ambiguity, or responding to crises, is simply above the Drones' pay grade. It is not so much that they are resistant to it; they are incapable of it.

A good example was the rise of the SUV. It is not as if the public demanded ever-larger land barges to convey their families to the cottage, to the mall, or to the soccer game. Instead, the higher margins of the vehicles drove the automakers to create an artificial demand for a vehicle, which met artificial, as opposed to functional, needs.

The U.S. Congress and Senate enabled automakers by providing them with legislative loopholes that made the SUV more economical for the consumer, and by extension, more profitable for the manufacturers. The 1975 Energy Policy and Conservation Act allowed sport utility vehicles to be classified as "light trucks," which are allowed much higher miles-per-gallon ratings. This gave automakers a loophole big enough to drive through with a whole new generation of gas-guzzling SUVs. This double standard has made a mockery of all subsequent efforts to ratchet up U.S. fuel efficiency standards, exempting a huge segment of the car market from tighter rules.

Large corporations will pay lip service to treating their employees as individuals, but this is only a way to bait the hook. Once the applicant is inside, the entire emphasis is on submerging the new recruit into the groupthink of the company. Training programs and team-building seminars are thinly veiled attempts to indoctrinate the individual into the corporate culture. They provide another benefit to the corporation; namely, the opportunities to pre-screen the applicants in order to determine which ones are the Drones, the Players, and the potential troublemakers. The Drones will make up the rank and file. The Players will be destined for leadership. The troublemakers will soon find themselves elsewhere.

This process begins in business school with the recruitment of the best and brightest. The curriculum and the entrance standards are tailored to their needs, as they are the end users of the product these schools turn out. Effectively, the corporation is out-sourcing its management training, with the taxpayer and the applicants picking up the tab.

Masters

Nicolai walked into the café. Up till now we had only communicated over the phone, with our conversations often extending for hours. The topics either centered around my model, or his algorithm; peppered with political and philosophical commentary.

I recognized him immediately: the unkempt hair, the discordant arrangement of clothing that looked as if they had been pulled out of a cupboard in the dark, the distracted, yet intense expression on his face—all gave him away.

I stood up and waved. His face lit up, a smile twinkled in his eyes, suddenly softening his weathered Slavic features, giving them a child-like expression. At first, the conversation was a bit stilted as each of us got our bearings. After the halting start, the exchange took wing. Someone watching from another table would have seen two middle aged men, excitedly gesticulating, passionately pressing their points, trying to make the other really "get" the essence that lay behind their thoughts. Each ready with their response before the other had a chance to finish their diatribe.

Nikolai is a Master. In the world of Players with their smooth, even delivery, careful selection of topics, designer clothes, and impeccable grooming, he finds himself completely lost. Small talk is simply beyond the capacity of the Master. The clever banter, name- dropping, references to the last golf game you had or restaurant you tried, makes no sense to him. When Nicolai speaks, it is to convey a point. When he finds your arguments compelling, he will happily say so. If he does not, which is the more likely case; Nicolai will let you know—bluntly! The weather may change, fashions may change, the times may change, but Nikolai remains steadfastly the same!

One of the great hidden costs of the Player Culture, with its obsession with impressions and perceptions, is the brain drain it creates. The Nicolais of this world—brilliant, original, and authentic—are among its first casualties. They are the Mozarts whom the Salieris must discredit and marginalize, lest their own mediocrity and perfidy be brought to light.

In the short term this does not pose much of a problem. The Master is easily replaced by someone else, far less brilliant, marginally competent, but infinitely more compliant. The problem arises when there is a crisis, or a major shift in the business playing field. In these cases it is not enough to follow prescribed practice as stated in the company manual, splice a few sound bytes together to make a strategy, or bamboozle the market with a few marketing tricks. In such times, real substantive thinking is required, something of which the Players, and those in their entourage, are simply incapable.

Such periods were the exception in the past, today they are the rule. Now when we need them the most, the thinkers are nowhere to be found, having been removed from the playing field long ago.

Let us examine each of the types of Master to see why they are a threat to the Players.

The Thinker

Firstly, we have the creative thinkers. This refers to abstract thinkers such as mathematicians and philosophers. These thinkers have the ability to penetrate beyond the surface to divine the hidden patterns that lie beneath. For them the world of theoretical first principles is far more real than the surface reality we encounter in our daily lives. The thinkers typically present as introverted, distracted, absent minded, or overly intense. They talk about ideas and concepts rather than facts, or people. They are unable to engage in small talk of any kind, severely handicapping them at cocktail parties or around the water cooler at work.

Such thinkers can be of use to the Players in solving specific problems; however, the Players will never let them anywhere near the inner circle where the real power resides. Often they will be well paid, but the clear understanding at all times is that the Players are in charge. If this condition is violated (the thinker wishing to be an equal partner), the Players will simply get rid of them, to the point of cutting off their nose to spite their face.

The Free Spirit

The second category of Master is the maverick, the free spirit. Free spirits are by their very nature non-compliant. As such they are totally unsuitable to the square box structure that sustains the Player Culture. In the large organizational environment they are typically subversive, irreverent, and contemptuous of dogma and authority. The free spirit is typically the first casualty of the rigid control structure. Such people are regarded as being unmanageable. Typically, when they are let go, the charges levied against them are that they are difficult to work with, not team players, or simply do not "fit in."

The Individual with Moral Character

The thinkers and free spirits being the most obvious threats to the player culture are sidelined at the start. However, there is one more purge, which takes place far more gradually. This is the purge of those of strong moral character, those who have integrity, those with a strong moral rudder, and tell it as they see it.

Such people innately know what right action is and require no external roadmap to guide them in moral questions. Typically, they will not talk about morality, nor see themselves as especially noble; they will simply see the alternative, that being to follow the herd, as unacceptable.

In environments where a high degree of conformity is demanded, such people do not fare well. The morality of the herd, which characterizes the majority in any large social grouping, applies rules selectively. Rank within the company, clique affiliations, etc., weigh heavily in deciding what degree of moral obligation is owed to whom. This kind of subjective morality is not something that the authentically moral person will countenance, as for them morality is blind to such distinctions, and is not tempered by expediency. This will cause them to be regarded as "unreliable" by those Players higher up the ladder, thus limiting their opportunity for advancement.

DIAGRAM 4: THREE TYPES OF ANTI-PLAYERS

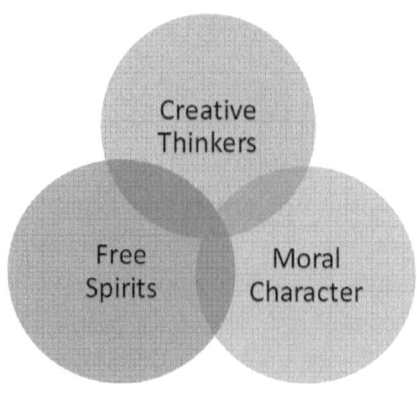

Summary

Each of the categories of Master shares a common trait—an insight into a hidden order. Each of the three experiences this differently. For the thinker it is the essential blueprint that lies embedded inside the structure of all things. The free spirit experiences this as the genie of inspiration. Meanwhile, the individual of substance is guided by a moral rudder that supersedes logic—an innate ability to distinguish between right and wrong.

This shared connection to a higher calling at once sets the Masters apart from others and places them beyond the influence of the Players. This creates a dilemma for the Players on two levels.

First, the Players by nature need absolute control. The Masters are by definition wild cards; so long as they are at large the Players' control is not absolute and their hold over the environment is not fully secured. This then places the Players in an untenable position.

Second, the Masters may be oblivious to the enmity that the Players feel towards them. As they are focused on something other than the social reality around them, the notion that they should be perceived as a threat by anyone would strike them as absurd. Also, the Players' preoccupation with their hidden game is incomprehensible to the Masters. From the Master's perspective, to invest so much time and energy in such a mundane pursuit is simply unimaginable. This makes the Master easy prey for the Player, who is often able to finesse them and get them out the door with the Master none the wiser.

Third, there is yet one more very practical reason for the Players to conspire against the Masters. The corporate cult is the glue that holds the Circle Square Pattern in place. The distinguishing characteristic of a cult, that which makes it a cult in the first place, is the uniformity of thinking and behavior among its members. This single-mindedness is a type of trance—a robotic state of awareness, somewhere between sleep and consciousness.

This trance aspect is at once the trump and the Achilles' heel of the Players. On the one hand, once this trance is firmly in place, all the Players need do is let it run. With a cult in place, the company runs on autopilot, and the situation takes care of itself. On the other hand, in its absence, sooner or later those in the company would surely come to the realization that they have been played. Therefore, it is absolutely imperative from the Players' perspective that this trance be maintained, regardless of the impact to the bottom line as a result of lack of market feedback, unresponsiveness, or brain drain.

For the corporate culture to be effective, all within the company must buy in. Even if just one individual in the crowd resists accepting the shared reality prescribed by the Players, there is the risk that this doubt could spread like a virus through the organization. The Masters, as we've described earlier, by their very nature, are unlikely to fully buy in, as they are too firmly grounded in their own reality. This is not willfulness on their part, so much as a matter of basic temperament. The Master is the silent witness, the one in the crowd who knows the Players for what they are—nothing more than bombastic impostors. As such, the Master is, by their very existence, a mortal threat to the dominance of the Players.

Therefore, it is not just out of cupidity but from practical necessity that the Players must move the Masters as far away from the line of power as possible. In situations where a Master possesses technical expertise, or a creative talent that is indispensable to the firm, they will be retained. However, even in such cases they are tucked away in some specialty department where their exposure to the main line staff can be kept to a minimum.

5. THE CIRCLE SQUARE PATTERN

Once the population of Players in the upper ranks reaches critical mass, a tipping point is reached after which the organization becomes subsumed by a Player Culture. The Circle Square Pattern (CSP) is the generic structure created by the Player Culture. It is a natural extension of two characteristic traits of the narcissistic personality style characteristic of the Players:

- Entitlement – Considering themselves to be accountable to no one.
- Control – The need to hold all those below them accountable.

The three elements that support the structure are an elitist inner circle, a rigid control structure, and a dogmatic corporate culture. Presented as a formula, it would appear as the following:

$$CSP = E + R + D$$

Where:
E = Elitism
R = Rigidity
D = Dogma

The Circle

The senior managers, being Players have a natural tendency towards an autocratic, aristocratic management style. They tend to distance themselves from the day-to-day running of the company, preferring instead to devote their energy towards "strategy." In order to secure their position at the top and avoid scrutiny, the Players need to minimize transparency. This is done in four ways:

1. Political Correctness

The environment is split into two. Most in the company take the stated values of the organization at face value and attempt to conform to them. Meanwhile, those in the inner circle pay lip service to these values while pursuing their own agenda.

2. Physical Separation

This two-caste effect is also achieved via physical segregation. The executive offices are typically physically located either well away from the administrative and operational facilities, or housed in an altogether different location. There is no "open door" policy in the Player-driven organization, and access to executives is tightly controlled by those in their entourage. Even written communication must pass through channels prescribed by organizational protocol.

3. Restricted Access to Information

There is limited transparency around all of the key decisions made in the company. A general secretiveness pervades the organization, with a reluctance to disclose information of any kind. The typical justification for this opaqueness is protecting the company's proprietary interests by ensuring that sensitive information does not fall into the hands of outside parties.

4. Skewing the Executive Selection Process

The only way to preserve this two-tiered game is to have restricted access to the inner circle. This is achieved by promoting only those who are likely to fit in to the upper ranks. This will usually entail stacking the deck in the informal selection criteria to ensure that only the right sort of candidate is put forward.

The best way to ensure loyalty of those in the circle is through complicity. Some form of malfeasance is the typical mechanism used to achieve this result. These days this is done legally by manipulating the corporate governance system to yield consistently high bonuses to those in the Inner Circle irrespective of the true economic performance of the firm. This acts as the glue that holds the group together. Should anyone suddenly find their conscience, they will invariably discover that they are in too deep to blow the whistle.

The Square

The autocratic style of the Players creates a corporate governance system that is rigid, complex and dogmatic, and becoming increasingly so with the passage of time. A heavy emphasis is placed on compliance and accountability, discouraging free-thinking and personal initiative in the process.

The organizational structure is left in place. On the surface, it looks the same and continues to direct traffic—transactions and information—within the organization. However, the rules are being subtly adapted in such a way that all are held strictly accountable through a highly defined chain of command. Meanwhile, those in the inner circle are accountable to no one but themselves. Such a rigid, strict culture creates an atmosphere that is tense and anxious. Fear and distrust now begin to permeate the organization, which psychologically destabilizes those within the ranks. This process is insidious, its gradual onset making it imperceptible to most within the company. In order for the culture to be fully effective, there needs to be unquestioning obedience.

All must regard the rules and regulations as moral laws. By extension the company, and the senior management, must be seen as inherently moral. This explains why the Players go to such great lengths to appear morally righteous and "nice." This is the true basis for political correctness—the need to shroud their agenda with a mantle of propriety.

The Corporate Cult

Over a century ago, the brilliant French philosopher and sociologist Gustave LeBon in his book The Crowd described crowd psychology in exhaustive detail. As LeBon illustrated, once a group of individuals are transformed into a cohesive crowd—be it a team, a panel of experts, a jury, or a mob in the street—they have become a single entity, thinking and acting with one mind and as one individual. Through the transformation of a group of individuals within the company into a collection, the CSP is now complete. It has now achieved the requisite structural integrity to assure sustainability. The two elements—the circle and the square—are now tightly locked into place through their mutual interdependency.

Players need to close the circle in order to conceal their agenda, as much as their shortcomings. The square—the complex labyrinth of quasi-moral dogma necessary to keep all in their places—creates an atmosphere of anxiety and confusion, and directs attention away from those individuals, far from being the best and brightest, who are running the company. Finally, the Crowd Effect has the impact of imprinting the square on the collective mind of the crowd. This means that with the crowd polices itself, without any assistance from formal authority. It's an organization effectively running on autopilot.

This perfect ecosystem is at once the strength of the CSP while also being its major weakness. Stability of the system introduces rigidity to the organization, which grows with time into complete paralysis and fossilization.

The Circle Square structure draws certain types of personalities towards it while repelling others. Those who are best suited to the kind of rigid, linear approach that the Players have towards management are Drones—those who are compliant by nature, have a low tolerance of ambiguity, and have a very strong need for order and authority in their world. Meanwhile, certain other personality types—those who find the conformity and politics oppressive—will withdraw or be passed over for promotion. These would include creative thinkers, free spirits, and those with strong, individualized moral convictions—all those who march to a beat of a different drummer. These are the potential Masters.

The corporate culture associated with this rigidity is a kind of Drone culture. This then sets the tone for the entire organization. This Drone culture functions adequately in relatively static situations, however, once the environment starts to become more variable these Drones are simply not able to adapt to the new conditions. Their programming is directed at accommodating conditions in the past, not in the future.

Within this culture, functional areas become progressively more specialized. Instead of integrating and synthesizing information from several areas, these days many people's mental functioning is more akin to data processing. The result is that their ability to respond to the unforeseen is severely restricted, their response being confined to a limited range of pre-programmed strategies. This makes for employees who may be highly efficient in the classical sense, but are not particularly effective at getting the job done. In the past, the focus was upon producing more; now it must be on producing intelligently.

DIAGRAM 5: THE CIRCLE-SQUARE PATTERN

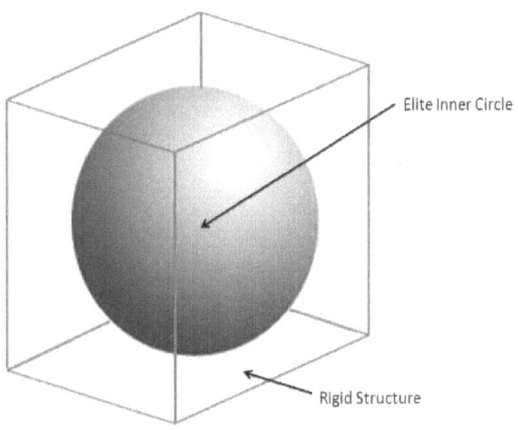

Elite Inner Circle

Rigid Structure

Inevitable Decline

Over time, the grandiosity of the Players grows, creating an increasing pressure on the company to expand its reach. This causes a series of problems. Firstly, the impetus to expand puts pressure on the organization to grow in ways that stray from the core business, diluting its competitive advantages. This then places additional stress on financial and operational controls, as well as on lines of communication within the firm.

The inherent rigidity of the organization responds to this additional stress by becoming still more restrictive, which further aggravates the problem. This feeds back into the system by creating further motivation to expand in order to balance itself. The removal of any lingering Masters means that in times of crisis there are none on staff who are capable of really analyzing the problems, coming up with original and creative solutions, or who have the strength of character to be the bearer of bad tidings and contradict the groupthink. This further limits the range of movement open to senior management in dealing with situations as they arise. Not being up to the task, the Players have a natural tendency to retreat further into their ivory towers, driving the downward spiral faster still.

DIAGRAM 6: THE CORPORATE CULT

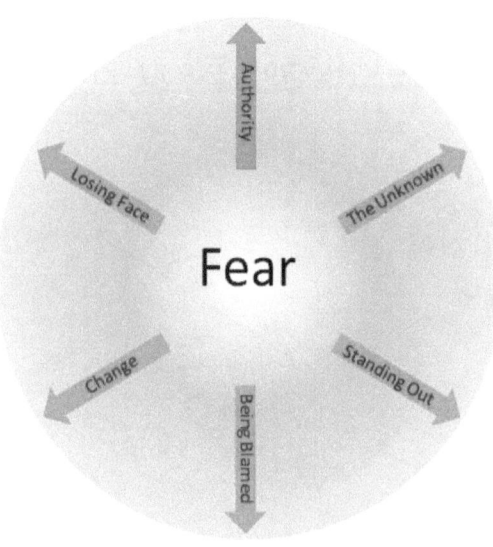

The absence of any self-correcting mechanism that might counteract this tendency creates a momentum that is irreversible. Employees become increasingly disillusioned with the tediousness of their work, the backstabbing politics, and the phlegmatic attitude of those at the top. This translates to poor morale, the lowering of standards of quality and service, absenteeism, and high turnover. Ultimately it manifests in a kind of "blowback" wherein the employees become subversive and spiteful, leading to petty theft and even outright sabotage. The cumulative effect is a downward spiral that is, like a vortex, drawing more and more resources into it, at an ever-increasing rate. The result is that by the time the company does fail, which beyond a certain point becomes inevitable, it may take down partners and stakeholders with it.

Summary

Take any piece of iron and leave it outside, exposed to the elements, and it will oxidize and produce rust. Over time the rust will spread and penetrate the surface of the material, progressively eroding and ultimately compromising its structural integrity.

Similarly, the Circle Square Pattern is not a random configuration that happens from time to time under the presence of certain specialized conditions. It is instead the path of least resistance for any organizational culture. In the absence of intervening factors, over the fullness of time, it is the inevitable outcome.

DIAGRAM 7: IMPACT OF THE CIRCLE-SQUARE PATTERN

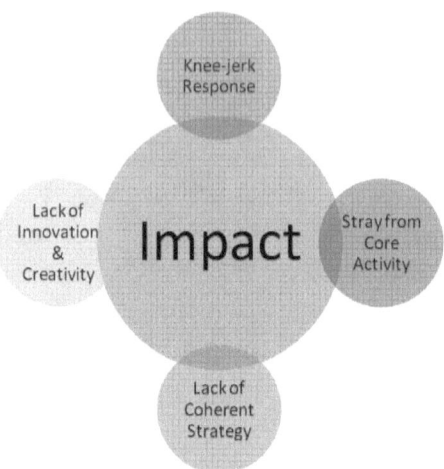

These three phases – the formation of the closed inner clique (Circle), the rigid control structure (Square), and the corporate Drone culture— represent a progression. Once all three elements are in place, the loop is closed and the company is locked into a certain set way of operating, and a kind of groupthink begins to grip the organization, bringing with it conformity in thought and behavior. The organization is effectively on autopilot, rigid and insular. It becomes a world unto itself.

Each of the three elements in the pattern derives from a pre-existent weakness within the traditional system. The Circle is an extension of the tendency for tiers within the organization to compete with, and mistrust, one another. The Square arises from the preoccupation with maintaining control. Finally, the Drone culture results from the insular nature of the large organizational culture; demanding absolute loyalty from those in management, forcing individuals to place their fealty to the company ahead of all else – friends, family, and even personal integrity. By enlisting these as the pillars that support the Player Culture, the Players are committed to keeping them in place, and strengthening them to the extent possible. The downside of this is that it severely restricts management's range of movement in responding to changing market conditions, and the crises they generate.

6. THE SZEGED CASE STUDY

In the early nineteen-nineties, I had the interesting experience of being the CEO of a paprika and meat processing plant in southern Hungary. The circuitous route that led me to this position is a story in itself, but suffice to say, that I was mandated by a major Hungarian bank, the firm's main creditor, to turn the company around.

This episode gave me a very personal immersion into the world of Players and Drones, and revealed to me the daily workings of the Circle Square Pattern. Here I found the rigid hierarchy, the shameless pursuit of short-term personal profits, and indeed the willful denial of reality that are the hallmarks of the Mesozoic organization.

The project began as you might expect to see in any business school case study. I went to Szeged, the city where the plant was located, and in true textbook fashion I spent my time learning about the company. This activity consisted primarily of countless meetings with the top brass, major customers, and suppliers, with the goal of developing a strategic plan that would lead them into the future. This process continued for several months, during which time the existing nomenklatura that was firmly entrenched, were exceedingly courteous and helpful to me in answering all my questions and unhesitatingly accommodating all my requests.

Szeged is about a two-and-a-half-hour train ride from the capital city, Budapest, the place where I was living at the time. Each Monday morning, I would board the 6:30 train bound for Szeged, remain there for the week, and take a return train Friday afternoon. As this was during the winter months, every Monday morning when I departed from Budapest, it was still the dead of night. The train would take me across the southern plains of Hungary to my destination. In dawn's first light, the mist-covered plains were dimly lit by a purplish light. By the time I reached Szeged, the sun had risen, the mist had receded; the day had begun.

Even though Hungary is a relatively small country, and the physical distance between Budapest and Szeged is not that great, the actual experience of being in Szeged is as if one were in a totally separate universe. To the outer world, Budapest was the capital of a former Russian satellite; the hub of a highly centralized socialist economy. The reality on the ground was quite different. The major cities in the various regions of the country, Szeged among them, were the real seats of power outside the capital.

Like little fiefdoms, each had their own parochial aristocracies. Lip service was paid to the administrators in Budapest, but the local brass enjoyed a relatively free hand in the management of their affairs. In the case of the Szeged plant, this meant that the local branch was very much running the show with next to no interference from head office.

Every Monday morning I would arrive in Szeged, and proceed to the front of the station to meet the company driver who was always there to meet me and take me to the office. Akos, the driver, would say, "I trust you had a pleasant journey, Sir." I would reply in the affirmative, and then he would convey me in silence, to the plant.

Akos was always punctual. But one morning when I arrived at the station he was nowhere in sight. After waiting for a few minutes I set out on foot, taking the shorter route across the railway tracks. All the while, the feeling was growing inside me that something was off. As I was negotiating the fences and tracks, I was experiencing a general sense of dread descend upon me. A knot was steadily tightening in the pit of my stomach, growing steadily as I approached the factory.

Finally, I arrived at the plant. The gatekeeper greeted me with the same formal nod of the head, as he always did. However, this time something in his manner made me feel that he was surprised to see me.

The plant was comprised of a random scattering of buildings chaotically spread over an area of several acres. There was a small administrative building that was the nerve centre of the complex, and located near the entrance to the compound. The executive offices were on the upper floor. I proceeded to the administrative building. As I opened the entry door, I saw a huge crowd of workers, standing shoulder to shoulder, squeezed into the staircase and foyer. Immediately, a murmur started to work its way through the crowd that, "Mr. Hardy was here." It struck me as strange that they even knew my name.

In the several months that I had been at the company, I had never encountered any of the workers directly. The closest contact I had had was seeing them at their various machines during a site tour on which I was escorted during my initial days at the company.

As I approached the staircase, the workers moved aside to make a pathway for me up the middle. Upon reaching the upper landing, a stocky woman in her thirties approached me. "I am Marta Kovacs, the union representative," she said. I introduced myself in turn and asked Marta what was going on. "Last Friday was pay day. When we opened our envelopes we found that our pay had been cut by a third." Marta went on: "No one notified me, or anyone else. We have come here to talk to someone in charge, but the only person here is Magdi [the VP of finance], and she is not willing to talk to us. Will you speak with us, Mr. Hardy?"

After a few moments of hesitation, I agreed to the request, and we decided that the best venue for the exchange was the building next door, which housed the cafeteria. Once the workers were all assembled in the cafeteria, I gave a short speech in which I described my mandate and my position as the bank's representative. I discovered that my decision-making powers had been greatly exaggerated to the workers by the senior management, and that their current predicament had been laid at my feet. I explained that their current picture of the situation was a misunderstanding, and I asked to speak with the line managers so that I might gain a better understanding of what was really going on.

The shop steward then arranged for the line managers, a group approximately twenty in size, to convene with me in an adjoining room. The steward joined us as well. We assembled around a large table, and I listened. We came from different worlds, but one thing we shared in common was the shock, and outrage at having been duped.

Over the course of the next several hours, I found out more about the company and its situation than I had learned in several months of meeting with the executives. I saw then that I had been purposefully cocooned in a world of paper reports, lunches and speeches. Here, for the first time, reality was staring me in the face. However, far more importantly, something magical took place in that little room with twenty odd people crammed around a lunch table.

Every one of those managers in attendance had lived their entire lives under the Communist regime. The socialist doublespeak in which everything is justified in relation to the cause, the people, or the party, was all that they had experienced in their entire working lives. This was the first time that a person in a position of authority, even if, as it turned out it was only perceived authority, was genuinely interested in their experiences, in their insights, in what they had to say.

What ensued was not a choreographed staff meeting, but instead, an authentic exchange between human beings. I have no doubt that the incredible feeling of hope and camaraderie, which I experienced, was shared by everyone in that room. For a brief window in time, we all shared a belief that a better, kinder, saner world was possible.

The fact that the old guard soon got wind of what was cooking, and in short order managed to quash the nascent rebellion, is lamentable. However, what we experienced in that room could not be undone, un-remembered, by any of us. The very fact that a collection of people, in a moment in time, could feel that level of hope and connection means that this was more than an aberration or a collective illusion. There in Szeged, with people who had lived their lives in the greyest of environments, who had no objective basis to believe that life should promise anything different, I witnessed a flare ignite in each and every one of them as they came to believe in the possibility of something better.

What this tells me is that the drive to connect to one's fellow man, to strive to create a better world for all of us to live in, is not a function of environmental conditioning, but is innate to each and every one of us. The human tragedy is that every organized society since the dawn of civilization has suppressed this impulse. This book is about the one great obstruction placed before human progress that has kept the vast majority of the human race in a state of penury since time immemorial—the Hidden Game.

The Saga Unfolds

When I first arrived in Szeged, the Budapest bank had recently forced the company into receivership and then appointed their local branch's assistant manager, Piroska Kiss, to be the receiver. An international consulting firm was actively courting the bank and Piroska. Their objective was to land a lucrative, long-term consulting contract, which would have had them effectively running the plant.

Piroska had no managerial experience, was gifted with neither charm, nor intelligence, nor the good sense to realize that she lacked the two. Temperamentally, she was ideally suited for her position: to take instructions and carry them out to the letter. Piroska was a Drone.

Piroska was in a predicament. Schroeder GmbH, a large German food importer, had loaned the company a room-sized industrial fridge. A truck had been sent from Germany expressly to collect the fridge. The truck was due to arrive any day, and she had no idea what she should do.

Schroeder was the major customer of the food conserve division, purchasing the majority of the plant's productive capacity. Recently, because of the financial difficulty the plant had found itself in, relations between the two companies had gone sour. Not wishing to risk the loss of a very expensive piece of equipment, Schroeder was anxious to have it back in their possession as soon as possible.

Recognizing Piroska's predicament as my opportunity, I suggested she do nothing. This notion stunned her, as she, like most people from behind the iron curtain, had a begrudging admiration for their old nemesis the Western businessperson. The idea of simply saying "no" to Schroeder would never have crossed her mind. I explained to Piroska, that as there was not to be any future business between the two, and we were in Hungary, as opposed to Germany, meant that Schroeder had very little in the way of immediate recourse, should she not comply with their demand. I went on to explain that Schroeder's business was critical to the plant and the fridge could be used as a bargaining chip to force Schroeder back to the negotiating table to extend their business relationship.

A few days later, the truck sent by Schroeder arrived at the gates of the plant. Piroska followed my instructions to the letter. She denied the truck access to the fridge while indicating openness to continuing our trading relationship. After a short standoff, which lasted a couple of days, Schroeder recalled their truck.

Piroska was so delighted with the assistance I provided her that she rewarded me with a consulting contract, as well as title "Chairman of the Board." I was to provide unspecified services for a very generous per diem for a period of three months. This, unbeknownst to me, had the effect of cutting the consulting firm off at the pass. After having invested months of politicking, their plans to take over the firm had been completely frustrated by an unknown appearing out of nowhere.

So far, so good! I had won. I had beaten the players. What I didn't know was that while I had won the battle, the war was far from over.

From that point onwards, Brian McDoon, a former Beverly Hills lawyer who was heading up the Budapest branch of the consulting firm, initiated a whisper campaign aimed at having me removed from my post. What this whisper campaign consisted of was Brian simply going about asking anybody even remotely connected to the Budapest Bank, the question: "Have you heard about the John Hardy problem at Szeged?" Up until that point, no one knew who John Hardy was, let alone knew that he should have single-handedly caused so much difficulty. However, by simply seeding the suggestion that there might indeed be a problem, it was enough to plant the notion in the close-knit banking circles that there was one.

Players are extremely adept at the use of innuendo. Direct assaults on a person's competence or character are risky, since the person may come up with an effective counter. With a whisper campaign, it is very difficult for the person targeted to pinpoint where the rumors originated, or what they are based upon. This makes defending the allegation difficult, and retaliation next to impossible.

In the meantime, I was surrounded by the old guard—the senior management who had been in place for over a decade. Compounding the problem, there was no provision in the budget for engaging any outside assistance on my part. The old guard was extremely effective at keeping me busy with high-level meetings, banquets, etc. Eventually, we reached a juncture, the details of which I will disclose in a later chapter, where it became clear that I could no longer be relied upon to fulfill the role they intended for me. This was to sit by dumbly while they carried on business as usual and in the event that something did go wrong, they had a foreigner to pin it on. Looking back, clearly even my victory in winning the contract was wholly illusory. In reality, I had been unwittingly drawn into a trap.

The Game is set up in such a way that no matter what the roll of the dice, the Players come out on top. This should not come as a surprise, since they are its architects. While everyone is busy occupying themselves with the task at hand, or trying to scratch their way up to the next rung on the ladder, or just scrounging in an attempt to keep their heads above water, the Players are sitting serenely in the eye of the hurricane coolly watching life spin around them.

The challenges facing the Szeged plant were numerous. It seems they were besieged on all sides. The plant produced two primary groups of products: paprika powder and canned meats. Both were hard hit by the liberalization of the market following the fall of communism.

On the paprika side, the paprika growers who were previously compelled to sell their crop to the plant could now sell directly to the market, driving the price of supply up and creating competition in the marketplace for the plant's own products. To make matters worse, the plant was in arrears to the supplier and thus was in an extremely weak position in attempting to negotiate new contracts in the future.

On the export front, they did not fare any better. Monimpex, the state-owned export company, had been covertly mixing inferior foreign strains of paprika in with the Hungarian paprika sold on the world market for years. The strategy worked well for a time, but eventually, when the market caught on to what they were up to, the Hungarian paprika was severely discounted.

The outlook for the canned meat situation was, if anything, even grimmer. New competitors had entered the market place, many of which were local entrepreneurs who had purchased bankrupt meat processing plants, similar to that of the Szeged plant. They had been able to purchase entire fully equipped plants for a fraction of the value of what their assets were worth, which meant that they enjoyed a built in cost advantage in competing with the existing plants.

Next, because of the subsidization of produce coming from the EEC, Danish beef was less expensive to buy than meat from the local slaughterhouses. Purchasing this meat was prohibited but with the appropriate payments to the local veterinary inspectors, in smaller quantities this was a viable "business strategy."

The bulk of the output had been sold to the German market via Schroeder GmbH. The factors detailed above had substantially eroded the profit margins and the Szeged plant had to explore other potential markets for their product. Unfortunately, the product was tailored to German tastes and the Hungarians found them to be inedible.

The remaining option, the Russian market, was not viable for two reasons: Firstly, the traditional customers could only pay in rubles, which were not freely convertible into hard currency at the time. Secondly, the only potential buyers, who possessed hard currency were the mafias. In Russia in the early 1990s there were two mafias. The first was the traditional organized criminal network, based in Chechnya. The second was the former KGB. Entering into business relations with either was highly problematic.

Finally, before the fall of communism the decision to shift resources away from paprika production towards meat production was originally driven by political, rather than economic, considerations. The Hungarian government was extremely thirsty for hard currency and any production facility that could produce for the Western market was rewarded with major bonuses the bulk of which were divided up between those in senior management. Therefore, despite the fact that the plant had no competitive edge in the meat processing industry, resources were shifted away from its specialty, paprika, and directed towards meat production. By the time I arrived onto the scene, over two thirds of the plant's resources were devoted to meat production.

Given all the factors confronting the plant, the real question was not: How do we make this plant profitable? It was instead: Why are we keeping it afloat at all? It was hemorrhaging money and there was nothing encouraging over the horizon. The answer to this question was political in nature. The Szeged plant was a major employer in the region, as well as a key customer for several of its suppliers. If it were to go down, it would take many of these small suppliers down with it, which would create ripples through the community. This was the official rationale behind the decision. Beneath the surface, however, there was a deeper, darker reason for its continued existence.

The Management Team

The first time I was introduced to the management team of the factory, was in the office of Imre Nagy, the president of the company.

The office was very spacious. It had the light wood paneling, a vast executive desk, and brown velour upholstered easy chairs and couch, which was the standard communist issue. This office could have been anywhere on the map from western Hungary to eastern Siberia.

Piroska introduced me to each member of the management team in turn. First was Imre, a huge bear of a man with a big head and heavy jowls. He was amiable enough, but there was an unmistakable apprehensiveness, which seeped through the jovial veneer. When we shook hands my hand disappeared inside his giant bear paw.

Next was Magdi, the VP-Finance. She was an attractive woman, no more than 40. She had maintained her excellent figure and one could imagine she would have been a striking beauty in her younger days. She wore a tightly fitted dress, which showed off her shapely legs. Magdi's demeanor was also a little nervous, but more cool and aloof than that of Imre. She had the cool, slightly dismissive air of a woman very much aware of her effect on men. The proximity with which she sat beside Imre, and the harmony of their movements indicated a connection that was more than collegial.

Finally was Istvan, the plant manager. He was slim, and athletic looking. His grey hair looked just coiffed. His steely blue eyes met my gaze, but revealed no emotion. In stark contrast with Imre who was dressed like most former communist executives in a brown shapeless suit, Istvan's dark blue suit was pressed and well cut. Istvan looked more like a German CEO than he did a plant manager in rural Hungary. Istvan was cool, icy cool. Magdi and Imre were Players. Istvan was a Puppeteer.

Another Agenda

When the Szeged plant could no longer service its debt obligations to its creditors, a medley of local suppliers as well as the Budapest Bank (BB), took control of the company. The mechanism they used to execute this was a variation of a debt-equity swap.

The idea behind the debt-equity swap is to replace bank debt with equity in the company, in order to improve liquidity and give the company some breathing room with which to pull themselves out of the mess they are in. What took place was an interesting variation on the theme, which did not involve the forgiving of any of the debt but gave BB a controlling interest in the plant. From the Hungarian perspective, they had greatly improved on a Western financial model. From any other perspective, it made no sense at all.

Fairly soon, I came to the realization that the way in which the bank's takeover was structured left the company in an untenable position. By taking the controlling interest in the company without forgiving the debt, BB was creating a lose/lose proposition. Unless the bank was prepared to do something to alleviate the pressure on the company, the situation was not sustainable.

In the West, this situation would almost certainly have led to liquidation. The plant was a major employer in the region supporting over one thousand workers and their families. In addition to this, were the myriad of suppliers linked to the plant figured in the equation as well. The closing of the plant would have created a tidal wave of unemployment and bankruptcies, which would have destabilized the local economy, already in a fragile state. Therefore, simply shutting the plant's doors and ceasing operations was an option which was not on the table. The bank was caught in limbo. On the one hand, they could not free themselves of the company, nor did they have the necessary commitment, both in terms of intellectual and financial capital, to set a course for the future.

It was in this regard that I wished to speak with the bank's president, Lajos Nagy. Mr. Nagy was at that time, not only the CEO of the Budapest

Bank, but was the head of the Budapest Stock Exchange as well. Later, he was to become the Finance Minister, as well as a serious contender for the post of prime minister. I felt confidant that a man of this stature and intelligence, when apprised of the situation, would help move us towards some sort of resolution.

Our meeting was in the morning. The secretary escorted me into the office. The CEO's office was a cavernous room with lofty ceilings, which dwarfed the standard communist-issue furniture. When I entered, Lajos got up from behind his desk and came out into the center of the room to greet me. He was very pleasant and engaging. Lajos bid me to sit down and the meeting began.

Lajos was very tall, well above six feet, but had a stoop, making him appear less imposing. He spoke softly and had an unassuming manner, which gave more the impression of a professor rather than a banking magnate.

I presented the situation as I saw it. Lajos listened attentively, nodding from time to time. When I finished my account of the situation, judging by his reaction thus far, I felt confident that we were very much on the same page. Lajos then responded by saying, "While I am fully sympathetic with the argument you are presenting, Mr. Hardy, unfortunately this situation is not in my hands, but under the jurisdiction of the local branch office."

I was dumbfounded! Up until then, there was every indication that Lajos was following the logic of my argument. In one fell swoop, the fate of a plant employing over one thousand people, was essentially dismissed as not his problem. It was as if the plant, the whole country for that matter, were being run by a chain of puppets. Piroska answered to Pal. Pal, it would have seemed, answered to Lajos. However, that was not the case. The question was, who was the puppeteer? Who was it that was pulling all the strings? I had encountered several of the players, but where was the master player at the hub of all this?

An Offer You Can't Refuse

Shortly after my meeting with Mr. Nagy, I met with Brian McDoon. He had suggested the meeting several weeks earlier when we met for the first time at an ex-pat function in Budapest.

The meeting was in Brian's elegant corner office with a view of the Danube. He was wearing a beautifully tailored suit, conservative, but obviously expensive shoes, French cuffed shirt with gold cufflinks, and a fashionable tie. Brian was formerly a Beverley Hills lawyer, as he took pains to let me know, and he looked every inch the part.

Brian was fully acquainted with the situation in Szeged, having spent several months courting the Budapest Bank, with a view to landing a major consulting contract at the Szeged plant. It seemed that he was poised to close the deal when I popped onto the scene, out of nowhere, and stole the deal out from under his nose.

After a brief conversation about life in general, our careers to that point, and the general situation at the plant, it came time for Brian to make his pitch. "Our firm," Brian said, "could provide you with a team of consultants who could analyze the plant from top to bottom, and really turn the company around."

After listening for a good while as he itemized the impressive array of expertise that could be placed at my disposal, I posed the simple question: "And what would my role be in all of this?"

I would be the lynchpin, he replied. He then proceeded to explain that I would retain my title and be the point man, the hub, around which all this spun. After a brief discussion, I told Brian that his offer was most interesting and I certainly would think about it. I took my leave.

On some level, I have to admit, the offer was tempting. It would have provided me with much needed resources, greatly increased the likelihood of success, as well as given me an excellent shot at a career path with an international firm doing similar work. The one fly in the ointment was

Brian. There was something about the smooth, slickness of Brian, which made me extremely uneasy. Though it all sounded nice, my suspicion was, that in reality, I would be nothing more than a puppet, not unlike Piroska, and Brian would be pulling the strings. The next question was regarding the likelihood of my contract being renewed once Brian's firm was fully settled in situ. I decided to decline the offer.

Waking Up

I still have a vivid recollection of the precise moment that I woke up to the realization that I had been played for a fool. At that point, I had already been at the plant for over a month. I was sitting in Magdi's office and we were reviewing the numbers to get a picture of what the unit profit was on each can of meat conserves sold.

Curiously, as we were going over the calculations we were always getting different results for the same product. One time it might be five fillers, the next time twelve fillers, and the following iteration would yield twenty-two fillers. In the span of only a few minutes, we had generated three vastly different results for the same product. When one took into consideration the fact that these conserves were being sold by the truckload with tens of thousands of units in a single truck, these differences extended into enormous differences in revenues for the plant. How was this possible?

With precisely that question in my mind, I looked at Magdi. The look she returned told the whole story. It was the look of a child with their hand caught in the cookie jar. My reaction in turn, was strong enough to make her flush. The fact was, we had no numbers. The company books were completely fictitious.

Magdi's reaction to my awakening was very telling. For a few long seconds we looked at each other in silence. Her look shifted from embarrassment, to fear, to defiance—all in the matter of a few seconds. This pattern represents the classic reaction of the Player upon being discovered. Being incapable of contrition their knee-jerk response is anger and defiance.

Our conversation ended there and I left her office to go into mine, which was immediately next to hers. I wasted no time and placed a call to Piroska at the bank. Upon apprising her of the shocking revelation, her reaction was remarkably cool. She simply said that the bank needed to get the financial projections regardless of what I discovered. When I pointed out the fact that with no reliable numbers to base it on such a projection was completely meaningless, this did not put the slightest dent in her resolve to get her numbers. The sensation was one of talking to a robot with one simple directive: to get the projections.

When I put down the phone, I was dumbfounded. How could the bank, the major creditor and now owner of the plant, be indifferent to the quality of the numbers supporting the projections, which were going to form the basis of the application sent to HO to acquire more funds? How, indeed!

What I did not realize at the time, but became abundantly clear soon afterwards, was that that which I had originally interpreted as a simple case of incompetence, was in fact, a fraud of massive proportions. This fraud was so pervasive that it included not just the plant's management, but that of the local bank branch as well.

As dark as the picture confronting management appeared, what was hidden beneath was darker still. The last two presidents of the company died under mysterious circumstances. The first, suddenly contracted an obscure form of cancer, the second hanged himself.

During the meeting with the line managers immediately following my address to the workers assembled in the cafeteria, something surfaced which placed the plant's situation in an entirely new light. A number of years ago, in what was presented as a progressive act of cost cutting, the nighttime security of the plant was contracted out to a small, private security firm. All were very satisfied with the company's performance. This security company not only did their job of protecting the plant, but also went well beyond the call of duty. They took the extra step of transporting meat and equipment en masse off the site and moving it to another location, owned by a privately held company in the business of selling canned meat conserves. The company was owned by a consortium, which, as it turned out, included the management of both the Szeged plant and the local branch of the Budapest Bank.

The company was indeed in difficult straits. Not only did they have to contend with all the problems related to the liberalization of the markets, they were being used as a front to funnel bank funds to a private meat processing company. Indeed the company's official dilemma was nothing more than a smoke screen to divert attention away from what was really going on.

In the meantime my role at the plant instead of being to guide the company out of this morass was to simply be a front for the old guard continuing business as usual, which had little to do with the real business at hand.

Exit Meeting

After the meeting with the workers, it was clear to all concerned that I could no longer be simply isolated. If they wished to prevent the possibility of further unrest at the plant the "John Hardy problem" had to be dealt with, and soon.

The bank manager requested that I meet him in his office. Actually, it was more of a summons. When we did meet, after a perfunctory exchange of niceties, we got down to the point straight away. Somehow, the branch manager, Pal, had gotten into his head that I was very much in need of a thorough dressing-down, and he was the one to do it. The tone he adopted with me was the one a vice-principal of a school might take with a student sent to him for discipline. In his mind, his trusted assistant, Piroska, could not be relied upon to deal with the problem and a stronger, steadier hand was required. Piroska, was a Drone; Pal was a Player.

As I failed to show Pal the deference and contrition he was seeking, very quickly the exchange became confrontational. The tone was going from bad to worse, regressing quickly from muted antipathy to outright disdain. At one point, when Pal had had more than he could take, he blurted out.

"There is nothing that I despise more than demagogues!" It seemed that falsehood of any kind was particularly offensive to Pal's refined sensibilities. Like most players, Pal lacked a keen sense of irony.

It looked as if we were at an impasse. Pal had expected that after the good dressing down I was to have received, I would meekly shrink away with my tail between my legs. In Pal's mind, I was either too stupid, or too arrogant to get the message—most probably both. He had to take a different tack.

Then something very interesting happened. As if a light had been switched on inside his head, Pal's entire demeanor took on a sudden change. With an engaging smile, he asked, "Would you consider taking the post of president of the company? Of course, the pay would be considerably lower than what you are receiving at present."

"I most certainly would," I replied.

"This will have to be decided by the board of the company. Both you and Imre can provide the board with your plans for the company, and then the board will decide who is the better qualified," said Paul.

Two weeks later the meeting took place in the boardroom. The board members included Piroska, representing the bank, as well as a number of local companies who had long- standing business relationships with the plant. One thing they all shared in common was that they were all clients of the Budapest Bank.

Imre and I each made our presentations, after which the board members were to cast their votes. The board patiently listened to our speeches after which they wasted little time in voting to award Imre the position, by unanimous consent. Afterwards Imre and I were called back into the room. Piroska, in presenting the board's position supported the group's decision with a couple of interesting comments.

Firstly, she commended Imre on having successfully negotiated an extension of the Schroeder contract. The fact that he was not in the room at the time the agreement was negotiated was somehow deemed to be beside the point.

Several months prior, shortly after we had forced the standoff over the industrial fridge, Schroeder came calling. As we were sitting in Imre's office, waiting for Herr Schumacher, the Schroeder representative, to arrive, the great bear of a man began moaning, complaining of indigestion. "I am not feeling well," he said. "I'm in no condition to have this meeting. I think I will take the rest of the day off." Imre then took his leave.

This then placed me in a somewhat uncomfortable situation. The only information I had on the Schroeder relationship was little anecdotes from Imre and Magdi, which I could hardly place much reliance upon. I was effectively going into the situation blind—but of course, that was the plan.

Soon after Imre's departure, Herr Schumacher arrived. We greeted each other formally, and I bade him sit down on the couch, and I joined him sitting in the adjacent chair. The Secretary came in to offer coffee and tea, as was customary, which was dutifully accepted. The meeting began. At first, the atmosphere was a little stiff, and he was a little taken aback that Imre was not in attendance. However, as time went on the ice broke and there seemed to be the beginning of a real rapport forming between us and. I explained my position to Herr Schumacher and what we, at the plant were hoping to achieve, after which he presented his firm's point of view.

"Schroeder GmbH," Herr Schumacher explained, "could easily source their products for far less from neighboring plants which have gone into bankruptcy and been purchased by local entrepreneurs." The only real counter I could offer was that the Szeged plant had been around for a long time and our respective firms enjoyed a long-standing business relationship, whereas these entrepreneurs were not likely to be reliable source of supply into the future.

I also pointed out to Herr Schumacher that there was a substantial credit in their favor on the inter-company accounts, which Schroeder would effectively forfeit if our relations were to end. Herr Schumacher went for the deal. As we parted company, he promised to send confirmation within the week.

Returning once again to the board meeting, Piroska went on to say that according to some vague international consulting body, which I had never heard of, my performance was deemed lacking.

What I found fascinating was not the decision itself but the need for an explanation. Everyone in the room knew the whole procedure to be nothing more than a comical pantomime with a foregone conclusion. Nonetheless, they all felt the need to sanctify it. It seemed that other than me, no one in the room saw the humor or irony in the situation.

This invisible pressure to maintain an aura of propriety and respectability, not so much for the outside world, but for themselves, is fascinating. The Players not only make up reality as they go along, they actually believe their own fantasy. If anything, they are the ones most taken in by their own press. The Players are as delusional in many respects as any inmate in a mental asylum. The only distinction is that they all share this delusion, and they seem to be able to convince us that it is true.

7. UTOPIA REVISITED

Formless Form

Several years ago when I first took up Tai Chi, my sifu (teacher) was someone whom I will call Andy. He was physically fit, had a confident demeanor, and performed the Tai Chi form with a vibrant athleticism. His form was smooth as he seamlessly transitioned from one position to another. He could go into low positions and then in an instant— seemingly effortlessly—transition to a high right-hand kick. As we in the class watched the exercises we were all in awe of Andy—his form, his cool, and his mystique. As the saying goes, "Women wanted him and men wanted to be him." Andy impressed us and he knew that his abilities gave him a certain emotional power over us. He was a rock star and we were his impressionable groupies.

A couple of years later, when I had gained some experience, I attended a Tai Chi tournament in which Tai Chi masters from all over North America performed demonstrations of various types of forms. One of these masters was a man whom I will call Jack. He wore glasses and had a boxy, squat build and a generally unassuming manner. Anyone passing him by in the street would not give him a second glance, and would probably take him for an accountant or a lab technician.

Jack began his form with the slightest, barely perceptible movements. As he continued, his movements were subtle—nothing special, but very smooth and seamless. His movements seemed to have a soupy, sort of cloudy quality to them. As Jack transitioned from one position to the next, it was as if just before the instant when one position would reveal itself, he would already be moving towards the next. To the casual bystander Jack's form seemed like a series of indistinct movements, and in fact not particularly Tai Chi-like.

However, what Jack's form did possess was a certain mass, a kind of energy that was absent in the other form. Watching it, you found yourself mesmerized and your eyes glued to the seamless progression of movements, not knowing quite why.

I realized that while Andy was a performer, Jack was a true Master. Years earlier, without having seen Jack's form and being somewhat naïve, for me Andy's Tai Chi had been the epitome of the art. But after having seen Jack's form, or more accurately experienced it, his version appeared to be the perfect image of serenity, style and competence. Just what one would expect to see in a Tai Chi (and this is a key point, for our expectations are the canvas upon which the social magician creates their illusions). After having seen Jack's form, Andy's version was but a pale imitation, nothing more than a parody of the real thing. Andy himself was little more than a poser.

Herein lays the essential difference between the Player and a Master: the form of the player is a hollow shell. The Players are illusionists, capable only of producing the appearance of reality, but without its requisite substance. They have become so numerous, as to have now defined today's zeitgeist—the Cult of Capitalism.

It is fair to ask: Is substance innate, or is it learned? The answer is that there needs to be an innate capacity within the individual. It is hard to conjecture what portion of the population possesses this capacity, particularly since the current paradigm, as defined by the game, has artificially reduced these numbers.

Environmental conditions must support it. Character is developed through adversity—the kind created not by the Circle Square pattern, but the natural pressure created by healthy competition. What is important is that the enemy is not inside, but outside the organization. By outside, we are referring only to outright competitors, and not to suppliers, customers, or strategic partners. Also, this dynamic, forward-looking, creative environment will generate a strong forward momentum in and of itself.

DIAGRAM 8: IMPACT OF REVERSING
THE CONTRA-SELECTION

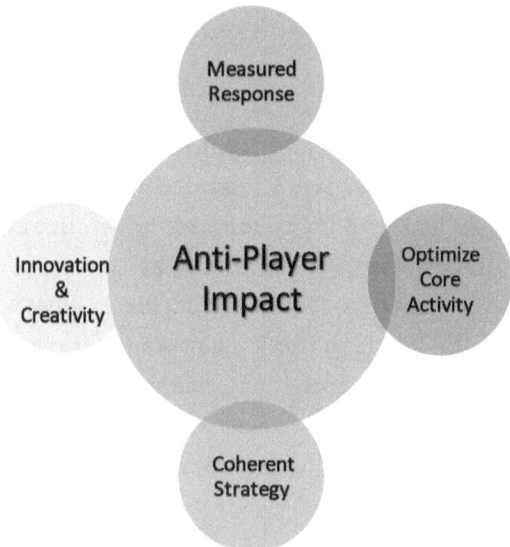

Core Principles

Masters function within a set of core principles. Why do we say "principles"? A principle is a law or rule that is understood by its users to be an essential characteristic of a system, or reflecting a system's designed purpose, and the effective operation or use of which would be impossible if any one of the principles were ignored. Principles are innate and elemental; they cannot be learned in a seminar. The three core principles are:

1. Mastery
2. Graciousness
3. Kindness

Mastery

The word "mastery," as it is in use today, connotes competence. Its original meaning went far beyond mere proficiency. It encompassed an understanding that transcended the application, extending to bedrock principles. It implied approaching activity with more than a mere skill set, requiring us to extend our scope of expertise to an art with a multitude of layers and nuances. As such, mastery in its pure sense is not attainable, but instead has remained an ideal towards which the practitioner of an art must continuously strive. Talent and perseverance are necessary ingredients for mastery, but by themselves are not enough. The path of mastery demands a strong moral character as well.

Perhaps the best-known modern example of this archaic approach to mastery is in the Japanese martial arts. The suffix "do," as in karate-do, or ju-do, translates to a life path that extends to every aspect of the devotees' lives, not just their comportment within the martial arts training facility (in Japanese, the dojo).

Mastery is innate to the human condition. We can find a variant of it in every culture, and in every epoch. Unlike the pop-psychology of today, that would have us deconstruct all human endeavors into a set of sub-routines, mastery is an indivisible gestalt. It defies operationalization. It cannot be broken down into skill sets and taught en masse. Invariably, it is passed from one generation to the next through apprenticeship. There would be innumerable parables and a dearth of textbooks. Rather than detailed verbal or written instruction, it entails hours upon hours of quiet observation. The only way to become a Master is to work beside one. One needs to be humble, patient, and hope that the Master deems you to be worthy enough for them to share their craft. This applies no less to the skills of leading a department than it does to creating a work of art, or learning a golf swing.

Mastery is not communicated as one of the values of the organization, but it is instead demonstrated by example. The ultimate expression of mastery is formless, wherein the art is practiced so smoothly, so elegantly, that the technique is invisible to the observer with an untrained eye.

Graciousness

I believe we are best to set our course towards an outer veneer that is gracious. Graciousness seems archaic in today's go-go, time-is-money, take-no-prisoners-world, and many would think of it as redundant and anachronistic. This is precisely why it can be so effective.

Firstly, graciousness involves demonstrating respect and consideration towards the other, placing the attention on them. It puts them at ease. Graciousness should not be confused with solicitousness. Its object is not to pander but to convey strength, poise and style.

Secondly, graciousness is a very effective way of taking control covertly. It enables us to set the tone of the interaction, in the same way that we can bring a horse to a trot by posting. Poise signifies authority, which induces the other to see us as the parent figure. We are all biologically programmed to please our parents and so without knowing it we are inducing the Player to seek our approval. Extreme vigilance is required in this respect because there is a danger of being perceived as patronizing which will generate the opposite result.

Thirdly, by being gracious we neutralize the Player. The arrows in their quiver—threatening, cajoling, coercing, and seducing—are all made to look clumsy and vulgar in their transparency when they are uniformly greeted by a civilized, benign response.

A famous example of this is an encounter between an infamous African dictator and a high- ranking British diplomat. The general made one absurd demand after another. Rather than enraging the megalomaniac by pointing out the absurdity of his requests, the diplomat simply, cordially offered him another cup of tea.

Finally, on a deeper level graciousness jams the Players' circuits. It neutralizes the Players by not giving them the anticipated reciprocal response, (be it anger or fear), which closes the loop that then drives the interaction. In the short run, the Players are likely to ramp up their activity, if nothing else, out of sheer frustration. However, if the outside Player stays the course they will most assuredly starve them of their psychic payoff and ultimately they will yield.

Kindness

I have reserved kindness for the end because it is the key to creating the atmosphere in which a company will thrive. Kindness, like grace or love, is a word that cannot be really defined, yet it transcends all social or cultural barriers. Therefore any attempt to give it some operational definition will only detract from it.

At the same time I believe there is real value in clarifying what kindness is not. Kindness is not niceness! Niceness is faux kindness. It is the essence of the political correctness that has completely pervaded the North American business culture. The key difference between the two is that kindness implies a genuine caring for the other, while niceness is directed towards looking good in order to gain some advantage, even if only perceived.

Niceness is perhaps even more toxic than outright nastiness because it crowds out kindness. Kindness requires an authentic connection between people. Therefore, in an environment pervaded by niceness, it is impossible to be kind. Conversely in oppressive, intolerant environments kindness, though rare, can exist.

The opposite is equally true. Where kindness prevails, niceness dare not show its ugly head. In an environment that is characterized by both sincere and courteous interaction, the politician, so adept at impression management, who thrives in today's business and political arena, has no room to maneuver. Those people, who are all form, but no substance, will be exposed for what they are. They will simply find no place in the new order. This in itself will be a tremendous cost savings to any company, as they will very quickly rid themselves of much of their ballast.

In their relations with their staff, senior management cannot just be perceived to be kind; they must actually be kind. This then trickles down through the organization, all the way to the mailroom and the receptionist at the front desk.

It is one thing to recognize what a healthy environment is when we encounter it; it is quite another to define it. Graciousness, spontaneity, kindness, inspiration, and resourcefulness all defy definition. Nor should we attempt to define them, since the moment we attempt to operationalize anything, it reduces it to empty form, a mere caricature of the qualities we wish to promote. Kindness becomes niceness; competence becomes compliance, while graciousness and spontaneity are both subsumed by political correctness.

Apprenticeship

When we in the West start learning Tai Chi we are usually baffled by all the exotic names given to the various positions that make up the form—"phoenix spreads its wings," "parting horse's mane," "cloud hands," etc. The explanation typically offered is that in past centuries this was the best way to communicate the movements to semi-literate Chinese. After having practiced the art for over a decade I see that it was far more than mere expediency that inspired this form of teaching.

Principles are better communicated through metaphors than through detailed logical explanations. They convey an image, a certain flavor which then provides coherence without creating restriction. This is very much at the heart of the approach.

The only way Mastery can be taught is through observation, long tedious hours devoted to learning the basics, and a slow steady progression from the rudimentary to the complex. In other words, Mastery is attained through apprenticeship!

Selecting the Leaders

It is evident that the leader in a culture of Mastery must be a completely different animal from the one that we find in the Control-Pressure

Paradigm (in other words, the one we typically find today). In such an organization managers will be more leaders then controllers. Character and substance would certainly be key success factors; and the selection criteria would include the following:

Character – The Master leads by example; therefore, they must have character in order to have credibility with their peers.

Experience – They need to be battle tested to ensure they fully comprehend the day-to-day reality of their domain, and can then empathize with those within their department.

Clarity of vision – They need to have a clear understanding of what they wish to achieve, while being flexible on how they wish to do it.

Inspiration – They need to be able to communicate their vision with passion, in the process inspiring those around them.

8. CONTROLS VS. CONSTRAINTS

The G20 Summit

Toronto is a pretty tame place; the kind of place where nothing ever happens. The population is calm, conservative; all are great believers in the sanctity of law and order. There are no radical groups of any size. Militancy of any kind is almost non-existent.

Thus on the surface, one might assume this would be an ideal place to hold the G20 Summit. Despite this, the security budget for the summit was projected at over $200 million—over six times the figure of the previous G20 Summit. The Canadian public perceived this sum as absurdly high, yet the politicians only gave the most perfunctory justification for the exorbitant bill. To add insult to injury, a couple of weeks prior to the event this sum inexplicably ballooned to nearly $1 billion. Major parts of the city were cordoned off like a high-security prison, all under the pretext of protecting the security of the participants in the conference.

After all the hoopla and expense, what was achieved? No one who lives in or around Toronto escaped being inconvenienced, frustrated and irritated by the oppressive security measures. Meanwhile, the professional anarchists, having no chance of getting anywhere near the summit events, not wishing to appear completely ineffectual, had to content themselves with smashing windows along the route of the demonstration. Finally, the city's business owners, normally the beneficiaries of such summits, lost money because the city was turned into a ghost town, as all who could, fled the city for the duration of the event.

All this demonstrates the inherent flaws in the assumption that security must be tight and in clear view to all to be effective. In making control overt, you give those who wish to subvert your efforts the blueprints to do it with. By making it blatant, the security measures morph into being symbols of oppression—intimidating those already inclined to be compliant, while provoking and providing public sympathy to the subversive elements in society. The vandalism, which would ordinarily have offended the average Canadian, became instead a kind of vicarious expression of their own frustration. The police, after spending an absolute fortune on security, came off appearing incompetent and ineffective. Finally, the taxpayers are saddled with a bill they did not support, for an event they never desired, all in aid of international initiatives no one really understands.

As we illustrated earlier in the book, there is an example of a completely different approach to security, one in which nearly perfect security is achieved imperceptibly: the Antwerp Diamond Exchange. The security is provided by undercover police disguised as shopkeepers, shoppers, a pair of lovers sitting at a café, etc. When the messengers meet, pouches are exchanged, with each then proceeding on their way. No paper changes hands; no inspection of the merchandise takes place. It is all done on trust.

During the centuries that this market has been in this square, great technological advances have been made in our society. We passed from the agricultural, through the industrial, into the electronic, and information ages. Nonetheless, this low-tech marketplace remains unsurpassed in the world, in terms of its efficiency, security and simplicity. The Antwerp Diamond Market is the model of control without restrictions. It is formless form at its finest. The flow of transactions is smooth and completely fluid, without compromising security. By way of contrast, the recent violence at the G20 summit in Toronto graphically illustrates the perils of taking the more traditional approach.

Tension

The Players, the CSP, and the Cult Effect are all inextricably linked. Therefore, provided that we are able to establish the existence of any one of these elements within the organization, we can expect to find the others as well.

Approaching the organization from the outside, the path of least resistance is to attempt to identify the atmosphere associated with the Circle Square Pattern. As it is all-pervasive, it is of no importance where we began our examination. This uniformity is one of the defining features of the Circle Square Pattern.

What then is the atmosphere characteristic of the pattern? Quite simply— tension! Tension is created by a combination of pressure and restriction. Pressure is generated by the Players and then translated and amplified by the crowd effect. The restrictions created by the Square squeeze the organization into a box and reinforce the labyrinth of regulations that those within the organization must navigate in order to get anything done.

With the passage of time, this tension grows, ultimately becoming the root cause of the organization's failure. This tension manifests in the attitudes of all those within the organization. It leaks out through their interactions with customers, suppliers, as well as with one another.

Therefore the path of least resistance for determining the existence of the pattern is to measure the tension within the organization. Having identified the existence of a pattern, it is fairly straightforward to verify the existence of its constituent elements.

How do we identify the Players and the Masters? Being a Player or a Master is much more than a role that we happen to choose for ourselves at some point in our lives. It is a way of being that is innate to the individual. A Player can no sooner become a Master than the Master a Player. Each has their own characteristic patterns of behavior that are reflected in their patterns of speech, choice of topics, and choice of metaphors. It also leaks out in their body language, extending even to the immediate impression each would make upon another on first acquaintance. The fact that they are polar opposites makes the task of creating a diagnostic that much easier since we can use one scale, one diagnostic, to identify both Players and Masters.

Dismantling the Square

Perhaps the best way to dismantle the square and create a structure that supports rather than inhibits those within the organization is to shift away from constraints and towards controls, as exemplified by the Antwerp Diamond Market.

One of the key advantages of this approach is that it will create an immediate impact on the organization. Transaction flow, and organizational responsiveness will increase, which will add to revenues. The investment in installing and maintaining controls will decrease. All this translates to a significant increase in profits for the organization.

At the same time, the tension in the organization will be reduced. This will immediately improve morale and contribute to a further improvement in responsiveness, in speed, degree and quality. The congenial, supportive environment will encourage risk taking on the part of employees—a necessary prerequisite for creativity and resourcefulness.

9. CONCLUSION

Change is natural. Change is good. Change is necessary. In the absence of intervening factors, change is the prevailing condition. Therefore, when the situation is stagnant, we have to look for a hidden dynamic that is preserving the status quo. This is the Circle Square Pattern.

The present paradigm of management, which itself lies within yet another paradigm, is based on a control pressure model. Control is exercised through compliance, and the pressure through accountability. The archetype of structure that supports this is the classical vertical hierarchy.

The greater socioeconomic context within which the control pressure model exists currently is capitalism. This model has become so pervasive in today's world that after the fall of socialism it is simply taken to be the way the world is. No longer is it a philosophy or a model; it has become ubiquitous, representing reality to the man on the street. Nonetheless, capitalism still remains a model, and a picture of reality based on a series of assumptions. Of course these assumptions have evolved into presuppositions and myths. Collectively, they become the noble ideas underpinning our present worldview. This then is the macro within which the micro of the control pressure model exists.

Now if we were to narrow the focus of our lens and bore deeply into the fabric of the control pressure model, we discover the hidden dynamic holds it in place. This is something the Circle Square Pattern (CSP).

The etiology of the CSP is a kind of perverted selection process in which those who are the best at appearing to be the best and the brightest displace those who are in actuality the best and brightest. The result is an organization that has all the outer appearance of competence and even excellence, while lacking any of its substance.

The ideal organization is the polar opposite of the control pressure model. In place of empty form we have formless form. In place of the individual departments or components of the system such as we have in the linear paradigm the emphasis is on the relationship between the elements. This is referred to as the Relationship Paradigm.

Supportive vs. Restrictive Structure

There is a role for structure; however, it is a far cry from the one in practice today. Without structure there is no freedom of expression and no creativity. Take the grammar out of language and what you have would be an idiotic stream of words that might be meaningful to the speaker, but would communicate nothing to the listeners (many would argue that this is precisely where we are headed these days).

Therefore we need some form of a structure to serve as kind of vessel used to convey meaning to others. When we are novices in a language, we experience this structure as confusing and distracting; inhibiting our ability to express ourselves freely. However, once we have mastered it, it is placed in the back of our minds; while we focus our attention on conveying the precise tone and meaning we wish to communicate.

Similarly, when we see Tai Chi being practiced by a throng of elders in a public park in China, meticulously following the same precise sequence of movements, performed at the same tempo, executed in exactly the same way. The impression is one of precise clockwork.

Now, if you are fortunate enough to see a master forming the same form by himself in a park, you would recognize the same form—but it would be somehow different. The movements would not be as distinct; they would bleed together and it would have a quality that might be described as soupy, or cloudy. They would have a quality that the others lacked—a certain smoothness, strength, depth, and energy that, while subtle, was immediately apparent.

And if you were to then see another master performing the same form on his own, the movements would yet again vary according to his particular style, while retaining the same core structure and depth of feeling.

If you were to witness either of these masters accosted by a hooligan you would likely witness a rapid sequence of indistinct movements that culminated in the hooligan being on the ground. Very likely you would not be able to recognize the specific movement in the form which was implemented by the master. This is formless form in practice.

Structure is meant to elevate us, to free us, not to confine us. In our world it has been subverted and has become the yoke to lock not just our bodies in place, but our minds and souls as well. The Player-and-Drone culture promotes a robotic mindset in which all are just going through the motions, with their minds parked elsewhere.

The problem arises when they have to deal with new and changing conditions—which these days takes place on a daily basis. They simply cannot cope! Having done their jobs mechanically for so long, when the situation varies, the employee simply has no idea of how to accommodate the new conditions.

Over the years, occupations have become progressively more specialized. Instead of integrating and synthesizing information from several areas, many people's mental functioning is more akin to data processing. The result is that their ability to respond to the unforeseen is severely restricted, with their response being confined to a limited range of pre-programmed strategies. This makes for employees who in the classical sense may be highly efficient, but are not particularly effective.

In the past, the focus was on producing more; now it must be on producing intelligently.

Mastery is one of the cornerstones of this alternative approach. The road to mastery is long and tedious, demanding endless hours of tedious repetition. The distinction between this repetition and that practiced by the assembly line worker is that for the artisan it is a milestone on the way to a deeper understanding, while for the assembly line worker there is no payoff whatsoever. Therefore for the line worker it has no meaning. The motivation for the artisan in enduring this monotony is the freedom, the self-respect, and the sense of accomplishment that mastery provides. Meanwhile, for the assembly line worker or the accounting clerk, there is no prize, no glory, no payoff whatsoever.

In the idealized town of Volterra, or in the Antwerp diamond market, the hidden structure that allows the system to function in such a fluent, seamless fashion is that everyone knows that everyone else in the choreography is able to play their part perfectly. Each individual's commitment to excellence is not just for their own sense of self-worth, but is also for the benefit of those around them, so as to not let down the others in their community. Unlike the pressurized conditions produced by the traditional model, this is the most natural condition. It would have existed in the early stages of our tribal development, and we see it among those, such as soldiers and firemen, who depend on each other's egoless confidence and empathetic support for their own survival.

DIAGRAM 9: KEY SUCCESS FACTORS
FOR MODERN ENVIRONMENT

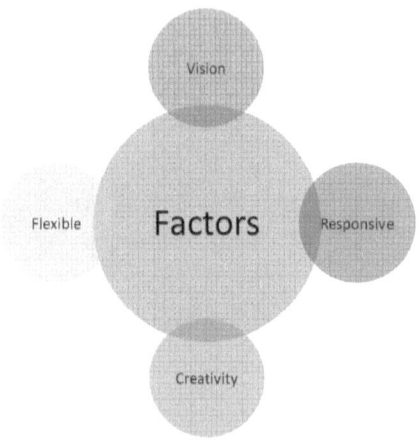

www.ingramcontent.com/pod-product-compliance
Lightning Source LLC
Chambersburg PA
CBHW030909180526
45163CB00004B/1771